The Headache Cookbook: A Tool for Migraine Self-Help

Patricia Holter Grasso
and
Jan Schaller Stump

Robert J. Brady Company
Bowie, Maryland 20715
A Prentice-Hall Publishing and Communications Company

Editor-in-Chief: David T. Culverwell
Acquisitions Editor: Richard A. Weimer
Production Editor: Karen A. Zack
Art Director: Don Sellers, AMI
Assistant Art Director: Bernard Vervin
Cover Photo: George Dodson
Typefaces: Trump Mediaeval (text), Optima (display)
Typesetting & Pasteup: Prestige Editorial and Graphics Services, Inc.
        Washington, D.C.
Printed by: R.R. Donnelley & Sons Co.
        Harrisonburg, Virginia

The Headache Cookbook: A Tool for Migraine Self-Help

Library of Congress Cataloging in Publication Data

Stump, Jan Schaller.
    The headache cookbook.

    1. Migraine—Diet therapy—Recipes.   I. Grasso,
Patricia Holter.   II. Title.
RC392.S88   1984   616.8'570654   83-15804
ISBN 0-89303-512-2
ISBN 0-89303-513-0 {CASE}
Prentice-Hall International, Inc., London
Prentice-Hall Canada, Inc., Scarborough, Ontario
Prentice-Hall of Australia, Pty., Ltd., Sydney
Prentice-Hall of India Private Limited, New Delhi
Prentice-Hall of Japan, Inc., Tokyo
Prentice-Hall of Southeast Asia Pte. Ltd., Singapore
Whitehall Books, Limited, Petone, New Zealand
Editora Prentice-Hall Do Brasil LTDA., Rio de Janeiro

Printed in the United States of America

84 85 86 87 88 89 90 91 92 93 94   10 9 8 7 6 5 4 3 2 1

CONTENTS

PREFACE

William J. Stump, M.D., Neurologist
and
Contributing Author

As a general neurologist, I frequently treat patients with migraine headaches and I am impressed by the variety of presentations of this disorder. A great deal of research has been performed on migraine; however, an exact understanding of the migraine process is still lacking. The role of various dietary substances in the production of migraine has been suspected for some time. However, specific research confirmation is still lacking and no one mechanism has achieved universal acceptance. I often use dietary restriction in combination with other modalities for the treatment of migraine. The general response has been very good, but many patients have found it difficult to follow a diet because of the limited dietary information available. It was this difficulty that lead to the development of this book.

ACKNOWLEDGMENTS

We would like to thank the following people for their contributions in making this book possible. A special thanks to our husbands who so willingly gave their continued support and love throughout the project.

William J. Stump, MD (Neurologist);
Harvey D. Grasso;
Robert Smith, M.D., Director, Headache Center, University of Cincinnati;
Mary Williams Dobrin, Patient Educator Coordinator, Headache Center,
    University of Cincinnati;
Ellen Fitz, R.D.;
Michele Muser Halligan, B.A., Editing;
Julie Hickey, Typist;
Kristi L. Lamberg, B.A.;
Jeananne Paul, M.A.;
Mary Lee Welling, R.N., M.A. Psych Nursing, Biofeedback Therapist;
Linda Schwartz, R.N.;
Patients from our Control Group;
1982 Cluster Headache Conference;
Darigold; William Sandine, Ph.D., Oregon State University;
Kraft Inc., Theresa Gargano, M.S. Research Nutritionist

INTRODUCTION

This cookbook is written for the headache sufferer, principally the diagnosed migraine person. It is to be used in conjunction with whatever treatment your doctor has prescribed and is not to be regarded as a cure-all or a substitute for your current treatment.

In the first section of our book we discuss possible causes of migraine, including physical, emotional, and drug- or food-induced. This is followed by a section on current treatment. Then, because our main emphasis is on diet and the role played by food in causing headaches, we have included a selection of "safe" foods and ways to make your shopping easier. We have gathered recipes containing these "safe" foods and set up both a Two-Week Sample Menu and a Holiday Planning section. These recipes are meant to be enjoyed not only by the migraine persons but also by their families and friends. Our clients who have used the Two-Week Sample Menu stated that not only did they feel better by reducing the frequency and number of headaches but also that their families felt that they ate better.

As you use our recipes you will notice that certain foods are missing. These include alcohol, table salt, monosodium glutamate (MSG), many dairy products, chocolate and nuts. Don't despair! There are still many healthful and delicious foods and seasonings available to you. Once your taste buds are retrained, you will enjoy the natural taste of foods and not even miss the salt. Also, you will have learned ways to improve not only your well-being but the general health of the entire family.

Initially there may be some concern that meal preparation may be time-consuming since most convenience foods are not for you. But once you have your basic stocks and dressings prepared and stored, meal preparation will be no more difficult than it was before. One thing that may help you to persevere is to remember that time spent cooking properly is time that will not be spent in bed later, recovering from a food-induced migraine. You may also look at the time spent cooking as money saved by not missing work. In addition, you will have more time to more fully enjoy your family and your life.

Since there is some disagreement regarding which foods are safe and which are not, remember that tyramine is the culprit most often associated with migraine attacks. Our "safe" food list is based on research done by Seymour Diamond, M.D., at his Headache Clinic in Chicago, and by John B. Brainard, M.D., in his private practice. Although research has been done on possible food links to migraine, no one has compiled a book of recipes and menus which would be helpful to the migraine person. For this reason we believe that our book is useful and hope that you find it so. One word of caution: if you suffer from food allergies, you have additional foods to be concerned about and should eliminate these foods from your list. Some of the foods included may affect some people and not others. In order to try out these foods you need to be migraine-free for two weeks, then add these foods one at a time. If you do not get a migraine in the next two days, it is safe to assume that this is a "safe" food and can be added to your diet.

What all migraine people must learn to do is to pay attention to their bodies and what happens to them when they eat certain foods. From this book we hope that you will learn that it is possible to enjoy good food with your family and friends in spite of your migraine problem, and also that by eating sensibly you can control your headaches and not have them controlling you and your life. The key is to pay attention to the messages that your body gives you and to respond by not repeating eating errors or reverting to older, easier ways. One final reminder: this is offered as an adjunct therapy, a self help, but not a cure. With this in mind we wish you well and hope that you enjoy using our book as much as we enjoyed compiling it.

Jan and Pat

Understanding
Migraine

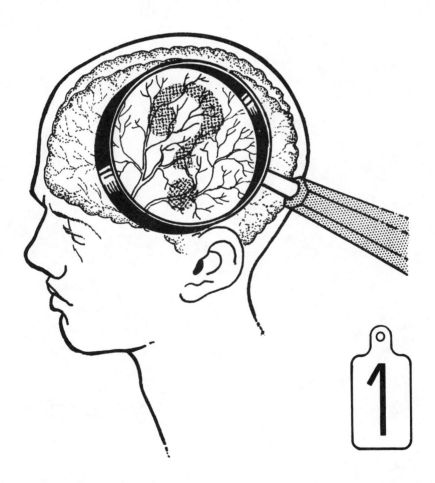

1

UNDERSTANDING MIGRAINE

It is likely that the word migraine is misused more than any other term in medicine. I would wager that all of us have had a friend or relative who has complained of a "migraine headache." Not all severe headaches can be described in this way, however, because there are many different causes of head pain. Migraine is only that head pain which is produced by dilation, or swelling, of the blood vessels of the head.

Migraine—Only One of Many Types of Head Pain

A question I am asked frequently is "Why does my head ache?" The answer to this question is difficult because there are many structures inside and outside of the skull that can cause pain in the head and neck area. Diseases of the eyes, the sinuses and the teeth are common sources of headache, for example. Pain can be produced by pressure on the nerves inside and outside of the skull. The lining of the cavities of the brain as well as the covering of the brain are also sources of pain. Very often, pain comes from the neck, arising from either the muscles of the neck or from arthritic changes in the bones of the neck. The term migraine thus refers to only one of many possible types of headache—specifically, head pain resulting from the dilation of the blood vessels of the head.

Characteristics of Migraine

Although migraine is a complex disorder which can vary greatly from individual to individual, certain patterns in its occurrence are generally recognized. Migraine is a common problem; surveys have reported that between three to five percent of the population is troubled with the recurrent headaches. The condition can begin at any age but usually the onset is in late childhood or early adulthood. In women of child-bearing age, almost twenty percent have migraine. The headaches tend to be more severe in the young and to decrease in intensity as patients age. There is no question that migraine is inherited, for as many as one-half of the patients report a family history of the disorder.

Clinical Types of Migraine

Migraine headaches can be divided into three general categories. Migraine is termed "classic" when the headache is preceded by visual problems or weakness or numbness on one side of the body. The headache then occurs on the opposite side of the head and is often described as "throbbing."

In the second category, "common" migraine, the events of the attack do not proceed in as clear a sequence and the visual complaints and/or symptoms of the extremities may not be a part of the headache. Furthermore, the pain may take place on both sides of the head; however, it too is usually described as throbbing in quality.

A third type of migraine is the infrequent but severe "cluster headache." These attacks come in groups, with periods of months or even years between the headache groups. The pain is always experienced on one side of the head and is often associated with tearing and redness of the eye and stuffiness of the nose on the affected side. Despite their severity, cluster headaches usually last for less than an hour. The headache may happen two or four times during a night, often recurring at the same time in a twenty-four hour period.

In all three categories—classic, common and cluster headaches—the outstanding characteristic of migraine is the recurrent nature of the headaches.

"Triggers" of Migraine Attack

People who experience migraine headaches have a greater sensitivity to various agents or stimuli, and their blood vessels are more reactive than normal. Anyone can have a migraine under certain conditions such as rapid pressure change, for example, but headaches are triggered more easily in the migraine sufferer. A number of "triggers" have been identified.

Stress has been linked to migraine and is probably the most common stimulus in our society. Trauma is another source; even a minor bump on the head may set off a migraine. When a patient wakes from sleep with a headache, it appears that the attack was brought on by the shifting patterns of brain activity which accompany sleep. A sudden change in the weather can sometimes be the culprit.

Another group of triggers has to do with eating habits. Missing a meal, for instance, may produce a headache due to low blood sugar. Some foods, especially those with a great deal of salt or certain chemicals, can bring on a headache, as can allergies to particular foods or other substances.

One more set of stimuli is focused on hormonal change. Many times migraine can be related to a woman's monthly menstrual cycle. In women patients, sixty percent have their headaches begin just before, during or after menses. A further connection with hormonal change is seen with the use of birth control pills, which often make migraine worse.

How the Blood Vessels React During Migraine

It is important to understand what happens to the blood vessels of the head when they react to one or more of the triggers or stimuli, some of which are discussed above. Within the blood vessel wall there are chemical compounds called "receptors." Once these receptors are triggered, the first action of the blood vessels is to constrict, or narrow, and therefore cause a decrease of blood flow to the area affected. Research has confirmed that it is the blood vessels outside of the skull which are chiefly at fault. This first phase is called "vasoconstriction."

The blood vessels inside the skull must also be involved, however, in order to explain the neurological symptoms—the visual difficulties, weakness and numbness of the extremities—which can appear during this phase. The duration of this period of constriction is highly variable. Some patients pass through it quickly and are barely aware of a change, while others may experience signs such as flashing lights or spots or vision loss for several hours. On occasion, the process may stop here and the blood vessels return to normal. If this happens, it is called an "aborted migrane."

Most of the time, the vasoconstriction phase is followed by a period of vasodilation, or swelling of the blood vessels. This dilation causes stretching of the blood vessel wall, thereby producing pain. Another factor of migraine pain is the collection of certain chemicals around the blood vessels during this phase. These chemicals make the vessels more sensitive to pain. The longer the period of dilation lasts, the more of these chemicals accumulate, and the more intense the pain becomes.

When the beating of the heart stretches the dilated vessels even further, the result is the pounding or throbbing sensation characteristically described in migraine headaches. The vasodilation phase may last from several minutes to several days and is often associated with nausea, vomiting, and possible abdominal pain, as well as sensitivity to light, sound or smell. Migraine has been related to a number of changes in the body as a whole; in fact, the entire chemical structure of the body is altered during an attack. These changes account for the generalized total body complaints that accompany the headache.

Recovery is the last phase, and it may be slow. Even after the headache has ceased, the migraine patient may not return to "normal" for an additional twenty-four hours.

Treatment of Migraine

Much is known about migraine, and much can be done for the migraine patient, but there is no "cure" for the condition. There are multiple factors that combine to trigger an attack, and it is important to identify them. Treatment thus begins with a careful medical history taken by your physician. Several types of therapy are available in the treatment of the disorder. Many times a combination of methods is used to provide satisfactory control and to reduce side effects.

Because stress is so prevalent in our lives today, its control is the cornerstone of migraine treatment. The sources of stress are many, and can include our families, friends, jobs, and finances. Stress is not always related to unpleasant or uncomfortable events. It is possible for some patients to identify the contributing sources and to arrange their daily routines to reduce periods of tension. Although migraine patients are no more subject to stress than other people, they can react to it more strongly. Simple relaxation training can be applied to reduce the frequency and severity of headaches thus caused.

In addition to learning muscle relaxation techniques, some patients can learn to control body processes that were for many years thought to be beyond the individual's conscious control. This "mind over matter" approach is called biofeedback. In some cases, patients can learn to control the dilation of their blood vessels, thereby increasing blood flow and skin temperature in the hands, a condition which is associated with migraine recovery.

Various drugs are helpful in treating migraine. These medications fall into two broad groups. One group of drugs—ergotamines—is used to treat an acute attack. If administered early enough, the drugs can control pain by constricting the blood vessels. Ergotamines are available in many forms, including tablets, sprays, and injections.

Once a severe migraine is established, however, the ergotamines are rarely useful. If the headache reaches this point, medications to control vomiting are necessary, as are pain relievers. One type of pain reliever is the non-narcotic group, such as aspirin, Darvon® and Tylenol®. If stronger relief is needed, narcotic medication may be appropriate. This powerful group of drugs is often given by injection. Because of their potential for addiction, they can be given only occasionally.

Recently a third group of drugs has been introduced. These are the preventive medications. When the frequency of the migraine is two or more attacks each month, this treatment may be useful. It is necessary that these medications be taken daily to prevent the headaches. The preventive drugs work to block the receptors of the blood vessel walls, and so keep the migraine from developing. One of the more effective medications in this group is propanolol.

Control of the headaches through diet is often a highly satisfactory approach. Since eating is such a common part of our daily activities, food can be overlooked as a source of one or more triggering agents. Many of the chemicals in food, however, can bring on a migraine attack. The chemical most often a factor is tyramine, found in such ordinary and widespread foods as cheese, chocolate and red wine. Salt, sugar, and other substances must also be considered. Careful review of one's diet and elimination or substitution of designated foods can improve migraine control.

In summary, it should now be clear that migraine is a complex reaction of the blood vessels of the head. The triggering agents are multiple and varied, and treatment must be tailored for each patient. It is important to identify which events and substances seem to cause the migraine headache so that they can be eliminated or their actions blocked. No one type of therapy will necessarily be successful for all patients; treatment often involves some trial and error. In most cases, migraine headaches can be effectively controlled. Your patience and persistence can be the most important elements in your treatment.

Possible Causes
of Migraine

POSSIBLE CAUSES OF MIGRAINE

There are probably as many theories about the cause of migraine as there are people who suffer from it. Some of these theories are supported by studies or research or both; some are beliefs held by the individuals who are victims of migraines. We will discuss five of these theories and possible roles each might play causing migraine.

Chemical Agents

In this section we will look at sodium chloride, caffeine and tyramine as the most common chemical agents associated with migraine.

Sodium chloride, ordinary table salt, is one of the most overused seasonings known to man. It has been added to nearly all prepared and processed foods and included in recipes for just about everything that we eat. The over-consumption of salt has been linked to many health problems, only one of which is headache. It is believed that salt in large amounts, as found in potato chips, pretzels and crackers, when taken on an empty stomach causes a sudden salt load on the body's system and sets the person up for a migraine. This theory has been studied and is supported by John B. Brainard, M.D. in his book, *Control of Migraine.* In addition, excess salt causes water retention which is also believed to increase one's susceptibility to migraines. We have based our recipes and the chapters on menu planning and dining out on this fact and have succeeded in creating many healthful and tasty recipes. For these reasons we encourage you to change your habits and follow the recipes given. In order to get used to the decreased salt taste, you should reduce the amount you normally use by one-half and then by one-half again until you have eliminated salt from your diet. One final word of caution: do not substitute sea salt for table salt. It is salt and acts on the body in the same manner.

Caffeine is a rather complex chemical to deal with, because it may be used to successfully treat migraine and may also trigger a migraine. Caffeine is a vasoconstrictor and this is its role in the treatment of migraine. However, since most of us drink tea and coffee in various amounts on a daily basis, we may run into a problem when we attempt to discontinue the use of these beverages. The withdrawal of caffeine may cause headaches in just about anyone, but the withdrawal headache may trigger a migraine attack in a person who is susceptible to migraines. For this reason, if you have migraines and feel the need to decrease the amount of caffeine that you use, do so on a gradual basis and avoid the danger of a rebound headache setting the stage for a migraine attack. You will notice that we suggest the use of only one to two cups of coffee or tea per day in our menus and then decaffeinated whenever possible. The use of soft drinks with caffeine is discouraged for some of the same reasons, but also because cola drinks have the same base as chocolate and therefore are not tolerated by the migraine person. We do not suggest the use of diet-type drinks because of their high sodium content.

Tyramine, a vasoactive monoamine, is believed to be one of the chief causes of migraines. Tyramine is present in most dairy products, particularly cheeses, which are such a large part of the American diet. Thus, most migraine persons will need to change their eating habits in order to avoid this chemical. In addition to being present in cheese, tyramine coupled with histamine is present in wines. Histamine is a vasodilator and acts by expanding the blood vessels, especially those in the head; this may trigger a migraine. Red wine is considered the most dangerous of the wines, although any wine can precipitate a migraine. This is also true of other alcoholic beverages, all of which act as vasodilators and for this reason must be avoided. We have used some white wines in cooking and have developed some drinks using vodka, which has been demonstrated to be safe for the migraine person to use in moderation.

Fatigue

Fatigue is a symptom felt by the migraine person as a signal of a possible impending migraine attack. This is most often observed in the person with the "weekend" headache. What is believed to happen is that after going full speed all week and instead of listening to their body saying "I'm tired," the person pushes on to that Friday night activity and sets the stage for a weekend migraine headache. You may observe this phenomenon in yourself if you keep a chart of your headaches and notice that they only seem to occur on weekends. The way to avoid this is to rest on Friday evening after a busy week and then do that special activity on Saturday or Sunday. This way you should be able to avoid missing out on weekend fun and be in control of your headaches, not have the headache controlling you. We do not much support the psychological theory that the weekend migraine is caused by guilt, not allowing yourself to have a good time or feeling guilty if you do.

Premenstrual

The *premenstrual time* in the female migraine person may be one of the times when women are most highly susceptible to a migraine attack. During this time a combination of factors come into play. First, most women report at least a two to five pound weight gain. This is caused by water retention. Then there are also a number of women who complain of fatigue during this time. This may be caused by the weight gain, the blood loss or the period of hyperactivity that some women experience just prior to their periods. With all of these factors present at the same time as high hormonal changes, it is easy to understand why this is such a critical time for the female migraine person. A few common-sense methods may help a woman through this time and aid her in avoiding a migraine headache. Number one, once again, is the reduction and elimination of your salt intake. Remember, it is the salt that retains the fluid. Now strange as it may seem, the way to combat this is to increase your intake of water by up to six to eight glasses per day, depending on your size. The water is flushed through the body and increases the reduction of salt in the system, thus decreasing the retained fluids. This theory has been demonstrated by John J. Brainard, M.D., in his private practice. And finally there is the awareness of the fatigue and once again listening to your body and responding to its needs.

Medications

In this section we will discuss some of the more common offenders such as birth control pills, nitroglycerin, vitamins and minerals and propanolol. Due to the complexity of the treatment of migraine, it is important that you are treated for it by only one doctor who knows you and your case. It is also important that this doctor be aware of all of the medications that you are taking, including those prescribed by other doctors as well as those with which you are treating yourself. It is your responsibility to keep your headache doctor updated on any changes made in your medications. These changes could have an effect on the cause and/or pattern of your migraines. In order to be doubly safe, make sure that any doctor who treats you for anything is aware that you are diagnosed as suffering from migraines and what your current treatment is.

In addition to affecting various hormone levels in women *birth control pills* may also increase blood pressure and cause fluid retention. Headache is also a side effect experienced by some women on the pill. If you are a migraine female the combination of these factors may increase the severity and frequency of your migraine headaches. If the decreased salt intake and increased fluid (water) intake suggested in the previous section are successful in helping you avoid migraines, then the pill may not be a problem for you. If, however, you notice a change for the worse in your migraine pattern while you are taking the pill, you may want to discuss other methods of birth control with your doctor.

Nitroglycerin is a vasodilator used in the treatment of angina. It is also the main ingredient in the making of dynamite. One of the side effects of nitroglycerin is headache and this may be a more intense problem to those who are susceptible to migraines. As a medication, nitro is available as either a tablet or in paste form. The absorption through the dissolving of a tablet, through the skin, or in the air you breathe affects the entire system, thus possibly setting you up for a migraine headache. So here we are faced with a medication/chemical that is both useful and dangerous, but one that you need to be aware of for your own well-being.

Vitamins and minerals are generally self-prescribed medications. It is believed by some doctors that if we eat a properly balanced diet, we do not need vitamin supplements. Possibly most of us have been taking vitamins since childhood and generally believe that we feel better doing so. Therefore we want to alert you to the main danger of vitamin therapy, particularly megavitamin therapy—the high salt content coupled with the practice of taking vitamins on an empty stomach. If you find yourself getting a headache around mid-morning after taking your vitamins on an empty stomach, check the sodium content and try taking them after you have eaten. Or, if you are on a self-prescribed megavitamin regimen, try eliminating them completely. If, on the other hand, they have been prescribed by your doctor, discuss with him the sodium content and look for a possible substitute.

The last drug we will mention is a double-edged medication, the *propanolol group.* This medication is another vasodilator which is used mainly in the treatment of high blood pressure. Once again, one of the side effects is headache. However, it has recently been used in the treatment of migraines with mixed success. As William Stump, M.D. stated earlier in this book, he has recently used propanolol successfully with a number of his migraine patients. Also in a recent article published by Seymour Diamond, M.D., of the Diamond Headache Clinic, he reported success in a majority of patients treated with propanolol and even headache relief some months after treatment was discontinued. We mention this medication to alert you to the fact that some people may be helped by the same medication that may precipitate headaches in others.

Diet and Drink

Much of what the average person consumes on a day-to-day basis may be the source of their migraine problem. This problem may be compounded if you also suffer from food allergies. For this reason we have attempted to deal with both *migraine trigger foods* and *food allergy problems* when setting up our recipes and menus. There is some disagreement among professionals as to whether or not certain foods and beverages have a role in the cause of migraine. From our work with migraine patients, we believe that there is a direct link and that diet is one source over which the migraine person has control. It is for this reason that we have spent so much time attempting to make a part of your lives more comfortable and complete. There is further support for dietary causes and controls in work done by both Robert Kohlenberg, Ph.D., at the University of Washington and by Robert Smith, M.D., with Mary Dobrin at the Family Practice Center in Cincinnati.

In addition to the chemicals mentioned at the beginning of the chapter which are present in many common foods and beverages, you need to also be aware of other headache-causing foods, some of which are hidden in foods that we take for granted. These include foods like coconut, hot baked goods containing yeast, and MSG. Coconut is not always obvious in what you eat, since it is in foods such as non-dairy whipped toppings and prepared bottled salad dressings. Hot baked goods containing yeast are a possible headache source due to the chemical activity still happening in the yeast. You can still enjoy fresh baked goods as long as they are permitted to cool first. Toast does not have this chemical activity, so enjoy your toast or heated breads unless you have a wheat allergy.

As for MSG, it is in nearly every prepared food you can think of—soups, stuffings, packaged mixes, you name it and there is probably MSG in it. We have even found it in some seasonings such as lemon pepper. So you really need to know what you are eating if you want to avoid headaches.

Another possible source of migraine headaches is nuts, not just salted ones, but even the ones that you crack and eat out of a shell. Peanut butter is also in this category. The only possible exception is the macadamia nut, which we have included as a maybe in some of our recipes.

Soy sauce and baking soda also have high sodium contents and should be used sparingly, if at all.

A favorite of nearly everyone which must be avoided by the migraine person is chocolate. This is no doubt one of the most difficult foods to give up, especially if you are a "chocoholic" but you will find the sacrifice well worth it when you no longer suffer from a migraine.

Beverages are frequently taken as a filler on an empty stomach. As previously stated, tea and coffee should be used in moderation and whenever possible should be caffeine free. Soft drinks are for the most part not permitted, due to a) the chocolate base in cola drinks, and b) the high sodium content of diet drinks. Wines, beers and liquors have already been mentioned as problem beverages so we will just remind you that some may enjoy white wine and vodka when used in moderation.

Dairy products are in question if used uncooked and taken on an empty stomach. This eliminates ice cream, ice cream sodas, and milk shakes, but leaves baked custards.

In order to help you remember all of this we have written a chapter titled Categories of Safe Foods, and one titled Shopping Made Easier. If a particular food is not included in one of these chapters, chances are it was not considered a safe food. However, if it is a favorite of yours and you believe that we may have overlooked it, feel free to try it. Remember that you need to be migraine-free for two weeks before introducing a new food into your diet. Then wait at least 48 hours to see if you get a headache from it before deciding whether or not to include that particular food in your safe food list.

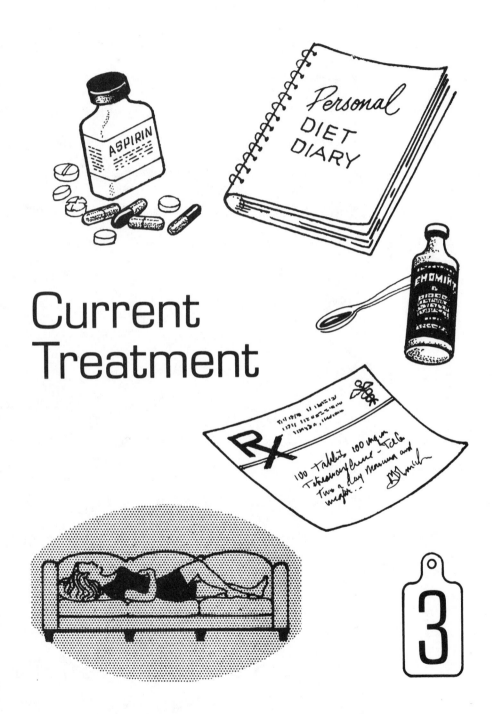

Current
Treatment

CURRENT TREATMENT

In this section we will review and elaborate on the current treatment modalities mentioned by William Stump, M.D., in his chapter, Understanding Migraine. This discussion will cover the three most popular and effective treatments in use today, popular not only with the physicians but also with the migraine patient.

Medications

Medication is no doubt the primary choice of treatment for migraine and the most popular. Treatment varies from doctor to doctor and from patient to patient, depending on the patient's need and response. Treatment with medication can also be rather complicated by the various side effects and the interaction with other medications. For this reason alone we cannot stress enough the importance of your doctor knowing *all* the medications that you are taking. In order to simplify this section we have divided medication treatment into four main categories.

Non-narcotic. This group includes aspirin, Bufferin® and Tylenol® and most over-the-counter medications that you can purchase without a prescription. It is usually suggested that these medications be taken when you first become aware of the headache and that you then go and lie down in a darkened room and try to relax until your headache passes. Some doctors also suggest the use of an ice pack at this time. It is important to remember that this form of treatment is for the pain caused by the migraine.

Prescription pain medications. This group includes such medications as Darvon® and Dolobid® in addition to narcotics. These medications also are only effective against the pain caused by a migraine and are not the treatment of choice. The problems with this group of medications are that they are only used after you already have a headache, and that the narcotics can be addictive. Also with this group it is necessary to go to a darkened room and lie down after taking the medication in order to give it a chance to help you. Usually the narcotics are used infrequently and as a last resort in the treatment of migraine.

Ergotamines. The medications in this group are vasoconstrictors and are available by prescription. They are usually prescribed in precise doses at specific times and must be taken thus at the onset of the migraine in order to abort, or stop, the headache. Let us remind you once again to pay attention to the signals your body gives you. It is believed that the ergotamines work by intercepting the second phase of the migraine, the vasodilation, which causes the pain. The one drawback to the use of ergotamines is that they do not work if you are into a full-blown migraine attack.

Propanolol. You may remember that this medication was mentioned in the last chapter as a possible cause of migraine. We mention it here because it is also being used quite effectively as a preventive form of treatment against migraines. It is believed that propanolol works by blocking the receptors of the blood vessels from the stimulus of a migraine trigger. In most cases the medication is initially taken three to four times a day. It is then gradually reduced and withdrawn in the hope that the patient will continue to have relief without the use of medication for a number of months. This medication is still being studied as a cure/treatment and, as stated before, it has met with mixed reviews.

As you may have observed from reading this section on medication, there is one thing that all medications have in common. That is the need for the patient to take the medications as prescribed. Also, most of the medications require that you retire to a darkened, quiet place until the medication takes effect. This may be a good thing for some people since it allows the body a chance to recoup. But for many this forced rest may be inconvenient or nearly impossible. Our strong suggestion is that you follow the doctor's instructions and take your medication at the first symptoms of a migraine in an attempt to avoid this lost time.

Biofeedback

Biofeedback is a popular therapy prescribed by some doctors as a form of stress management in the treatment of migraine headaches. Others use biofeedback in conjunction with diet control. Basically, biofeedback is a tool that the migraine person is trained to use before a migraine begins. It is believed that biofeedback works by moving the blood from the intercranial system to the peripheral system, thus preventing a migraine through interfering with the further expansion of the blood vessels in the head. Once taught this relaxation technique in the therapist's office over a ten to twelve hour period, the migraine person is able to practice this prevention technique at home or elsewhere. Biofeedback, as a treatment modality, has been used over the past fifteen or more years by many therapists. Currently, the combination of biofeedback and dietary control is being used successfully by Robert Kohlenberg, Ph.D., in his work with migraine patients. If used regularly by the migraine person, this can be an effective treatment and one in which the person is in control.

Diet Control

Diet control is a relatively new concept in the treatment of migraine headaches and is usually described as an adjunct therapy. It has also been used alone at the Family Practice Center in Cincinnati by Robert Smith, M.D., and Mary Dobrin, Patient Educator, where they have been treating migraine headaches with diet control for nearly two years. What diet control does is make you aware of two things: your eating habits and the role of certain foods in your migraine pattern. This is accomplished by keeping a diary of when and what you eat, thus developing a pattern of any food allergies and/or trigger foods and their relationship to the occurrence of your headaches. As with any type of treatment, some changes in your life style may be necessary. These changes most likely will involve lifelong eating patterns. However, based on feedback received from clients using diet control, these changes seem well worth the effort that it may take to make them. If your life has been controlled by your migraines, then we are sure that you are ready to take charge and that diet control is for you. With a firm resolution to make the necessary changes in order to be in control, let's move on to the next section—safe foods.

Food List

4

FOOD LIST

This section is designed to aid you in the selection of foods that are relatively safe from trigger substances. It is important to remember that you are not always dealing with a single food but with a cumulation of the various foods eaten throughout the day. You will need to experiment with the various foods listed to make certain that they are safe for you as an individual. You should be cautious when trying the "maybe" foods since some of them contain small amounts of tyramine, the culprit to all migraine sufferers; or some of them such as citrus products, onions and garlic have been found to be troublesome in studies conducted by other researchers. Any foods that you may question should be introduced into your diet one at a time and then only after a 2-week migraine-free period. Whenever possible we have included name brands to assist you, and have included a separate chapter called Shopping Made Easier. This food list used in conjunction with a diary should help you to remain relatively migraine-free. So enjoy what you can, safely.

Beverages

Try to stay within the parameters of the list as much as possible. The beverages you may want to experiment with are very light scotch, maybe white wine, beer or tequila. If you find that you can use beer or white wine then your recipes can be increased to include more exotic dishes. One final note: If you must indulge, most of the literature suggests that you limit yourself to two drinks, preferably with meals.

Apple juice
Carbonated water
Cider
Coffee
Ginger ale (pale, dry and golden)
Grape juice
Grapefruit juice
Lemon juice (Borden's reconstituted)
Lemonade
Lime juice
Limeade
Orange juice—maybe
Prune juice
Real Fruit Juice (Purple 100%, Red 100% and Golden 100% by Sun-Maid)
Root beer
Tang Breakfast Drink (Safeway brand)
Tea
Tomato juice—maybe (S&W Nutra Diet)
Vodka—maybe

Grains, Pastas and Cereals

Most of this group is safe, with the exception of cold cereals. The exception to the exception is puffed rice without salt. All cooked cereals are fine—just prepare them without using salt. You can enjoy rice, noodles (egg), and pasta. You may also have bread and rolls—but not hot from the oven since there is yeast activity still present that can cause headaches in anyone, even non-migraine persons.

Barley
Biscuit mix—maybe (Krusteaz)
Boston Brown Bread
Bran (plain)
Breads—maybe (warm bread not recommended because the yeast is still active)
Bread stuffing—maybe (OroWheat and Mrs. Wright's seasoned stuffing)
Bridgeford pizza dough
Buckwheat Pancake Mix
Bread sticks
Corn flour
Corn muffins
Corn bread—maybe
Cottonseed flour
Crackers (Nabisco—Wheatsworth stone ground; Kavli-Norwegian flat bread; RyKrisp-Natural, un-

salted snack cracker; Wasa-Crisp bread; Hol-Grain-Unsalted wafer-ets; Ak Mak, 100% stone ground sesame roman meal; Zwieback; Melba toast, white, rye and sesame by Old London-Bordens)

Croutons (Mrs. Wright's, plain and toasted)

Fish flour

Flour, cake (Softasilk)

Muffins (Howe)

Noodles (egg, Tuna Noodle Helper by Betty Crocker, homemade, chow mein)

Noodle Roni (Golden Grain, herb and butter ONLY)

Oats—maybe (Products such as rice and hot cereals, puffed rice without salt)

Rolls and buns (beware of the fresh hot yeast rolls). Refer to breads.

Rusk

Rye

Short bread

Spaghetti

Spanish rice (homemade)

Tapioca (Snack-pak, Hunts and Safeway brands)

Wheat (whole grain flour)

Wheat germ

Wild rice (raw, not the package mixes)

Yeast (this is not good while activated as in hot breads)

Zwieback (this is good crushed with butter for a pie crust)

Herbs, Spices and Condiments

Use fresh herbs and spices whenever possible to avoid the MSG that has been added to *many* of the dried products. Once again, read the labels carefully, as MSG is not necessary in any of these. The common condiments, mustard, catsup and mayonnaise, are all on the safe list—but avoid those made with wine. Also be cautious in your use of garlic and onions, as there have been mixed reports of difficulty with the use of these products. We have not had any of these reports from our clients.

Apple butter

Applesauce (Seneca)

Apples, crab apples spiced (S&W and Napoleon)

Bacon bits—maybe (Crown Colony or Schilling)

Barbecue sauce (Kraft)

Butter (unsalted)

Candied fruit (except for pineapple)

Catsup (most brands are fine)

Chives

Chili sauce

Cocktail sauce (Nalley, S&W and Heinz)

Cornstarch

Cotton seed oil
Cowpeas
Cranberry sauce with orange relish (homemade)
Cranberry sauce (canned, Ocean Spray and Safeway)
Cucumber pickles

Garlic clove—maybe
Gelatin
Grapefruit peel

Hollandaise sauce (Aunt Penneys)
Honey
Horseradish

Jams, jellies and preserves

Lard
Lemon peel

Macadamia nuts—maybe
Malt—dry
Margarine
Marmalade (citrus, plum)
Mayonnaise (Nalleys)
Molasses (to cook with)
Mushrooms
Mustard (prepared; read labels)

Oils (except olive and peanut)
Orange peel

Parsley
Peppers (hot or sweet)
Pickles (cucumber only)
Pimientos (canned)

Salad dressings, commercial—maybe (commercial, Miracle Whip, stay away from cheese types)
Sandwich spread (Nalleys)
Sapotes
Sesame seeds
Syrup (check labels for ingredients. Breakfast, *no* chocolate.)
Sorghum (all types)
Sugar
Sunflower seed kernels—maybe

Tartar sauce
Tomato catsup, chili sauce, paste, puree—maybe
Tofu (dressing and dip, homemade)

Vegetable cooking spray and oil
Vinegar (avoid wine types)

Water chestnuts—maybe
White sauce (Aunt Penneys or homemade)

Dairy Products

Food selection in this group is somewhat limited due to the milk intolerance of some migraine persons and the tyramine present in most cheeses. However, recipes requiring milk that is heated, such as in baked goods and custards, do not seem to cause a problem.

Cheese
Cottage cheese—maybe (low-fat)
Cream cheese—maybe
Cream—maybe
Cream substitutes (Dream Whip whipped cream. Read labels on all of the substitute packages and beware of coconut content.)
Milk, Cow's milk—maybe (cooked and used for cooking)

Milk, soybean, and soybean milk products

Milk, condensed sweetened—maybe

Non-dairy creamer (Mocha Mix)

(for coffee, cereal, fruit desserts and cooking)

Ricotta cheese—maybe (Precious)

Roe

Yogurt—maybe

Desserts

These are probably the easiest foods to remember—*no* chocolate, *no* nuts, *no* coconut. Also on the *no* list is whipped cream and the imitation white toppings. Other than that, eat whatever you like.

Brown betty
Bread pudding
Angel food cake
Caramel
Cottage pudding
Ginger bread (plain or with white raw or cooked icing)
Pound cake (homemade or Sara Lee)
Sponge cake (homemade)
White cake (with uncooked white icing and homemade)
Yellow cake (homemade)
Cake mix (check ingredients, no chocolate)
    Angel food
    Coffee cake
    Ginger bread
    Honey spice
    White
    Yellow
Icings (homemade)
    Caramel
    White (uncooked and boiled)
    Carob powder, cooked
Carob brownies (Manna Mixins)
Cookies, commercial (check the ingredients; homemade are the best)

Butter
Fig bars—maybe
Ginger snaps
Lady fingers
Marshmallow cookies
Molasses
Oatmeal with raisins—maybe
Raisin—maybe
Shortbread
Sugar (homemade)
Vanilla wafers
Sandwich cookies—maybe (check ingredients)
Cream puffs—maybe (depends on the cream filling)
Custard (boiled)
Danish pastry—maybe (do not eat hot pastry which contains yeast)
Doughnuts—maybe (do not eat fresh warm doughnuts)
Ices (water and lime)
Pastry shells
Pies (crust made with enriched flour is the best)
    Apple
    Banana custard—maybe
    Blackberry—maybe
    Blueberry—maybe
    Butterscotch

Cherry
Custard
Lemon chiffon and meringue
Mince—maybe
Peach
Pumpkin
Raisin—maybe
Rhubarb
Strawberry

Sweet potato
Prune whip
Puddings (homemade, imitation vanilla)
Rice pudding
Pudding (Snack Pack by Hunts and Safeway, such as tapioca and butterscotch)
Sherbet, orange

Fish

Nearly all frozen and fresh fish are safe foods; the most outstanding exception is preserved herring. Some of the fish named below are found only in certain areas of the country and are included to assist you in using what is plentiful and most available.

Abalone
Albacore
Bass
Buffalofish (suckers)
Bull head (raw)
Burbot (cod type)
Butterfish (raw)
Carp
Catfish (fresh water)
Clams
Cod and codfish cakes
Crab (blue, dungeness, rock and king, canned and fresh)
Crappie (white)
Crayfish
Croaker
Fish cakes (cooked and no MSG)
Fish loafs
Fish sticks (frozen, Mrs. Paul's fish fillets)
Flounder
Frog legs
Grouper

Haddock (frozen)
Hake
Halibut
Herring (raw)
Kingfish
Lobster
Mackerel
Muskellunge
Mussels
Perch
Pickerel (pike)
Pike
Pollock
Pompano
Rockfish
Salmon
Sand dab
Scallops
Sea bass
Shad
Shrimp (Scotch Buy frozen and breaded)
Smelt

Snail
Snapper (red and gray)
Sole
Squid
Sturgeon

Swordfish
Trout
Tuna
Whitefish

Fruits

This is an easy group. All fresh, frozen and canned fruits and fruit juices, with the exception of pineapple and coconut in any form or canned figs, may be used. However, some researchers have found clients who are sensitive to citrus products, so for this reason we recommend that you limit yourself to two servings per day.

Apples
Apricots
Bananas (overripe bananas are a maybe because there is a high tyramine content in the peel)
Blackberries
Blueberries
Boysenberries
Breadfruit (raw)
Cantalope
Cherries
Crab apples
Currants
Dates
Figs—maybe
Fruit cocktail—maybe (also the Hunts and Safeway brands of fruit cup snack packs)
Fruit salad (canned)
Gooseberries
Grapefruit—maybe
Grapes
Guava
Honeydew
Kumquat

Lemons—maybe
Limes—maybe
Loganberries
Loquats
Mandarin oranges
Mangos
Melons
Muskmelons
Oranges—maybe
Papayas
Peaches
Pears
Papaws
Plantains
Plums
Prickle pears
Prunes
Quinces
Raisins—maybe
Raspberries
Rhubarb
Strawberries
Tangerines—maybe
Watermelon

Meat, Fowl and Poultry

Fresh or frozen meat, fowl or poultry without breading may be safely eaten. Cured or preserved meats such as ham, hotdogs, cold cuts, dried beef, lox and for some migraine persons, even bacon, must be eliminated from your diet. Remember, if you think that you can eat some of the foods not listed below, use the 2-week migraine-free test when you decide to try one of them.

Beef
Brains
Cervelat—maybe (salami)
Chicken and gizzards
Ducks (domestic and wild)
Eggs
Egg Beaters (Fleischmann's)
Eel—American
Goose
Guinea hens
Hamburger or ground round beef
Heart
Kidney
Liver

Liver sausage or liverwurst—maybe
Meat loaf—maybe (no sausage)
Pancreas
Pheasant
Pork—maybe
Quail
Rabbit
Raccoon
Squab
Sweetbreads
Tongue
Tripe
Veal
Venison

Special Dishes

This section contains some favorites like waffles and pancakes, and even some surprises, such as pizza. These foods can be prepared from scratch or, in some cases, even from mixes. Experiment to find out which mixes are best suited for you.

Chili con carne (canned—maybe; homemade is better.)
Chop suey—maybe (homemade is better. No MSG.)
Chow mein—maybe (homemade is better. No MSG.)
Cole slaw—maybe
Corn fritters—maybe

Grits—maybe
Omelets—maybe
Pancakes—maybe (homemade and mixes)
Pizza—maybe
Popovers (homemade)
Soups—maybe (low sodium, Campbell's—split pea, chicken

with noodle, corn, tomato with tomato pieces, chunky vegetable beef. Homemade soups are better.)
Spanish rice (homemade)
Waffles (homemade)

Vegetables

All fresh vegetables with the exception of broad beans and possibly lima and navy beans are considered safe. Canned and frozen vegetables are questionable due to their high sodium content. There may be an exception in the canned line as Del Monte is introducing a new line of products. Read labels carefully.

Artichokes
Asparagus
Avocados—maybe
Bamboo shoots—maybe (raw)
Beans, lima—maybe
Beans (snap and yellow)
Beets and beet greens
Blackeyed peas
Broad beans—maybe (raw)
Cabbage
Carrots
Cauliflower
Celery
Chickory (endive)
Chick peas (garbanzo)
Collards
Corn
Cucumber
Dandelion greens
Eggplant
Kale
Kohlrabi
Leeks
Lentils
Lettuce
Lima beans—maybe

Mixed vegetables—maybe (fresh or frozen)
Mushrooms
Okra
Onions—maybe (blanched in water before using. Discard this water.)
Parsnips
Peas
Pea pods
Potatoes
Potato buds (instant, Betty Crocker)
Pumpkin
Radishes
Rutabagas
Soybeans
Spinach
Squash
Succotash—maybe
Sweet potatoes
Swiss chard
Taro
Tomatoes
Turnips
Turnip greens
Yams

Candy and Snacks

The selection here is somewhat limited because anything with obvious salt in it must be eliminated, as must any chocolate or nuts. This leaves you mostly with hard candy, plain nuts (maybe), gum drops and jelly beans.

Shopping
Made Easier

5

SHOPPING MADE EASIER

In order to help you shop with as few difficulties as possible, we have spent more than a few hours reading labels in two of the larger food chain stores in this area, and in our own pantries. We have examined a variety of foods and have listed brands that are considered safe according to our food list. This was done so that you do not think that convenience foods are completely out, and also to get you started on your own list. One word of caution: some companies do change their ingredients from time to time, so it pays to take a few minutes to read the ingredients, especially if there is a change in the packaging. Also, if you have any questions regarding ingredients, write to the company. There is a regulation titled "Consumer's Right To Know" which makes it easier for you to obtain the information that you need and you will find that most of the food companies are most helpful; at least this has been our experience. So here is a list with which to begin your shopping.

Breads and Crackers

Ak-Mak
Borden's—Old London Melba Toast, White (unsalted), Rye and Sesame
Brenner Poppy Seed Crackers
Hol Grain—unsalted whole wheat
Kavli—Flat bread
MJB Stuffing Plus—Chicken and Herb Butter with Wild Rice
Mrs. Wright's—toasted croutons
Roman Meal—(FFV) crackers
WASA
Wheatsworth—maybe

Dairy Substitutes

Cereal Blend
Dream Whip
D-Zerta whipped topping mix
Mocha Mix

Garnishes

S & W or Napoleon—Apple Rings and Special Apple Rings
Crown Colony or Schilling—Bacon Bits (used lightly)

Juices

S & W Nutradiet—Tomato or Vegetable Juice cocktail

Rice

MJB—Herb and Butter, White, Original Flavor Brown and Wild Rice

Sauces

Bar-b-que—Kraft
Seafood Cocktail—all except Crosse and Blackwell

Please note that only the specific foods mentioned under each brand are ones that are considered safe. So for example, not all rice products produced by MJB may be eaten—only those listed above. New to the market since this list was first composed are some salt-free vegetables by both Libby and Del Monte. If you must use canned vegetables, you will need to be creative with your seasonings as these are less flavorful than vegetables prepared with salt. Between this food list and those foods mentioned in the previous chapter, Categories of Safe Foods, you now have a good foundation for your new eating habits.

Two-Week
Sample Menu

6

TWO-WEEK SAMPLE MENU

Introduction

In order to get you started on a particular idea as to what you can eat, we have compiled a two-week menu. This will provide a guide as to what can be prepared and how each meal can be planned. We have consulted with a dietician to insure that each meal is well-balanced and suitable for the whole family. Wherever possible, we have suggested foods in common use, hopefully not disrupting your normal family dietary pattern any more than necessary. It is our feeling that by designing meals with the whole family in mind, it will be easier for you to follow the diet.

Although this is not a salt-free menu, we have tried to reduce the salt consumption to approximately half. Remember, this is only a guide. If you do not care for a particular food in the menu, then check through the food list for a suitable substitute.

In general we feel this two-week menu will provide you with a basis to initiate dietary control of your migraine and at the same time can be enjoyed by your entire family.

You will find that by planning your menu for two weeks, shopping will be much easier. Although you will want to take your food list along when you go shopping, it would be advisable to plan at home beforehand. By proceeding in this manner you will be more organized and your meals will be better balanced. As a bonus, your stress level will be reduced, which should in turn help reduce your chance of a headache. We all know what a headache meal-planning itself can be.

As you become more comfortable with the food list and menu planning, you can expand from the sample menu by substituting some of the "maybe" foods. The adjustments, however, should be made one step at a time. This will allow you to identify your specific "food triggers" and plan around them.

We are certain that after you have completed the first two weeks of the diet, you will have a new feeling of confidence in yourself and in your ability to control your headaches.

This two-week sample menu has been tried by diagnosed migraine persons and their families. The patients have reported a reduction in the number and severity of their headaches. Their families felt that the meals were tasty and satisfying. We have tested the recipes on our own families and friends, for taste, with good results. In fact, a year after we first tested the "Sample Menu," we are still getting positive feedback.

In conjunction with the use of the two-week sample menu it is a good idea to keep a complete diary. This diary should include all foods and the times that they were eaten and, of course, any headaches that occur. From this diary you may be able to notice a pattern in your headaches. Did they occur immediately after certain foods were eaten or hours later? Or were they present when you first got up or when you had not eaten for a while? There is some evidence that not eating is as dangerous for some people as eating the wrong foods. Another point to consider is any stress that may be present at the time of your headaches.

In order to record both your headache and stress levels we suggest that you use a scale of 0 to 10. A zero would be either no headache or no stress; one, a slight headache or slight amount of stress; and a ten, the worst possible headache or greatest amount of stress.

In order to help you compile your diary we have included a chart for you to complete each day.

Food and Headache Diary

1. In the proper space, record each time of day you eat. Include snacks.
2. We feel it is crucial to maintain a routine schedule every day and it is most important to stay with this schedule if you anticipate a long, hard week ahead.
3. If and when you get a headache, we would like you to record the time of its onset and, on a scale from 0-10, how you would rate its intensity.
4. We feel it is important at this time to determine what your stress factor was and, again, how you would rate this on a scale from 0-10.
5. We would like a record of the duration of the headache and if a medication was used to abort it.

Day/Date				
Time/Breakfast	Time/Lunch	Time/Dinner	Time/Snack	
Time of Headache	Intensity 0-10	Stress Factor 0-10	Duration of Headache	Medication (if any)

Day/Date				
Time/Breakfast	Time/Lunch	Time/Dinner	Time/Snack	
Time of Headache	Intensity 0-10	Stress Factor 0-10	Duration of Headache	Medication (if any)

Day/Date

Time/Breakfast	Time/Lunch	Time/Dinner	Time/Snack
Time of Headache	Intensity 0-10	Stress Factor 0-10	Duration of Headache	Medication (if any)

Day/Date

Time/Breakfast	Time/Lunch	Time/Dinner	Time/Snack
Time of Headache	Intensity 0-10	Stress Factor 0-10	Duration of Headache	Medication (if any)

A Questionnaire for the
Study of Migraine and Diet

A. Personal:

   1. Please answer the following questions. The first three are optional.
     a. Name:
     b. Address:
     c. Telephone No.:
     d. Age:
     e. Sex:
     f. Marital Status:
     g. Occupation:

B. Medical:

   1. How long have you had migraine headaches?

   2. At the present time how are your headaches being treated?

   3. Are you allergic to any foods? If so, could you please name them?

C. For the next two weeks we would like you to try to follow this diet plan. During this period we would like you to keep a diary of all the foods you eat and the time of day they are eaten. After this two-week period, we would like to you to answer the following questions:

   1. How many days did you stay on the diet?

   2. What was your reaction to the diet?

   3. What was your family's reaction to the diet?

   4. What was your headache pattern during this period?

   5. Did you deviate from the diet? If so, in what way?

   6. Were there any noticeable changes in your headache pattern? If so, what were they?

7. In what ways did the diet change your eating habits?

8. How did the diet affect the eating habits of your family?

9. Do you have any comments on the recipes?

10. Do you have any suggestions regarding the diet or the recipes? If so, would you please list them?

11. If you ate any foods not included on the diet, please list them and their effect.

12. Please list the medications used during this period.
    a.
    b.
    c.
    d.

13. Can you list any particular foods that trigger your headaches?

D. We would appreciate any comments you may have on the diet and the survey. Do you feel that the diet and/or a cookbook might be helpful to you in your day-to-day dealings with your migraine?

E. Would you please give us your comments on the recipes?
    1. Were the recipes difficult to follow? If so, in what way?

    2. Were they easy to follow?

    3. Do you have any recipes you might like to share with us?

    4. If we conducted other surveys in the future, would you be willing to assist us again?

F. Would you give us the privilege of printing your comments in a publication dealing with migraines? If so, please sign your name on the line below.

_____

We want to thank you for your cooperation and interest in helping us to find a way to make life a little bit easier for migraine sufferers and their families.

Menu

MONDAY

Breakfast
Broiled grapefruit

Toasted bagel with cream cheese*

Coffee or tea (decaffeinated for some)

—————

*Cream cheese is a "maybe" food.

Lunch
Barley-yogurt* soup, served hot or cold—garnished with croutons

Combination fruit salad, garnished with fruit salad dressing or mayonnaise

—————

*Yogurt is a "maybe" food.

Dinner
Wilted lettuce salad

Texas pot roast (includes onions, carrots, potatoes and mushrooms)

Whole wheat bread or rolls and butter

Warm gingerbread topped with applesauce

TUESDAY

Breakfast
Glass of juice (not pineapple)

Poached eggs

Creamed salmon on toast

Coffee or tea (decaffeinated for some)

Lunch
Cottage cheese and cantalope salad

Steamed broccoli spears with lemon juice

Rye cracker thins

Coffee or tea (decaffeinated for some)

Dinner
Cucumber and onion salad marinated in vinegar (white or cider) and spices

Kosher/beef frank* and vegetable bake (may substitute pork tenderloin)

Bread pudding topped with quick fruit dressing

Coffee or tea (decaffeinated for some)

---

*Kosher or all-beef franks do not contain MSG and can be toleratd by some.

WEDNESDAY

Breakfast
Fresh-squeezed orange juice

Baked mahi-mahi

Bran muffins

Coffee or tea (decaffeinated for some)

Lunch
Turkey-vege on an onion roll

Russian cream and fruit

Iced tea

Dinner
Spinach salad garnished with green onions and hard-cooked eggs

Pat's curried chicken

Green beans with basil

Rice pilaf

Banana loaf cake

Coffee or tea (decaffeinated for some)

THURSDAY

Breakfast

Hot applesauce with raisins and cinnamon

Stuffed french toast

Bacon (fresh)*

Coffee or tea (decaffeinated for some)

---

*Meat markets and the delicatessens of supermarkets carry fresh bacon.

Lunch

Sliced papaya with lime juice

Hot German potato salad

Cervelat (salami) slices*

Cucumber pickles**

Sour dough bread

Iced tea with lemon

---

*Cervelat can be bought at delicatessens and some supermarket chains.
**Do not substitute kosher dill pickles for cucumber pickles.

Dinner

Combo fruit salad with dressing

Relish tray—cucumbers, radishes, carrot and celery sticks

Hamburger deluxe, garnished with lettuce, tomatoes, onions, etc.

Julienne fries sprinkled with garlic powder

Zucchini carob cake

Soda water with cranberry juice and a lemon wedge, over ice

FRIDAY

Breakfast
Fried cinnamon apples

Soft-boiled eggs

Whole wheat muffins

Coffee or tea

Lunch
Bananas and mandarin orange sections

Tuna salad sandwich with lettuce on rye

Sliced tomatoes

Lemonade

Dinner
Green salad

Baked cod stuffed with vegetable-bread stuffing,
topped with creamed shrimp sauce

Buttered peas

Peach and pear compote

Coffee or tea (decaffeinated for some)

SATURDAY

Brunch
Avocado-grapefruit salad on lettuce with french dressing

Chicken-filled crepes

Doughnuts or sweet rolls, not caramel or nut-filled

Coffee or tea (decaffeinated for some)

Dinner
Antipasto

Vegetables a la grecque with tuna

Artichokes steamed in garlic and butter

French bread

Cherry torte

Fruit punch, coffee or tea (decaffeinated for some)

SUNDAY

Breakfast
Pancakes with syrup and minute-fried steaks

Eggs over easy

Apple cider, warmed

Lunch
Festive fruit salad

Stuffed pork or veal chops (bread stuffing)

Candied yams and apples

Cranberry sauce

Steamed asparagus with butter and pimientos

Parkerhouse rolls

Apple pie

Coffee or tea (decaffeinated for some)

Dinner
Hot roast beef sandwiches

American fried potatoes and onions

Roasted corn on the cob

Prune whip

Coffee or tea (decaffeinated for some)

MONDAY

Breakfast
Grapefruit juice

Homemade potato pancakes with yogurt

Soft-boiled egg

Coffee or tea (decaffeinated for some)

Lunch
Mom's vegetable-beef soup*

French roll

Ambrosia

Coffee or tea (decaffeinated for some)

---

*Mom's vegetable-beef soup cannot be started with soup starter because it contains MSG, and this is a no-no. Canned soups should not be used for any of the creamed recipes due to the sodium and milk in them.

Dinner
Sautéed liver and onions over toast (makes its own gravy)

Fresh green beans and mushrooms, buttered

Acorn squash cups

Pear sauce in lite syrup (Libby)

Carob chip cookies

Coffee or tea (decaffeinated for some)

TUESDAY

Breakfast
Tomato juice

Creamed egg cups and fresh bacon

Cinnamon toast

Coffee or tea (decaffeinated for some)

Lunch
Veggie sandwich on pita bread

Fruit with yogurt

Iced tea or limeade

Dinner
Chicken and dumplings

Buttered carrots with parsley

Zucchini salad

Fresh strawberry cake

Coffee or tea (decaffeinated for some)

WEDNESDAY

Breakfast
Orange sections

Hard-cooked egg

Muffin

Coffee or tea (decaffeinated for some)

Lunch
Avocado and crab salad on lettuce

Onion roll

Green grapes

Coffee or tea (decaffeinated for some)

Dinner
Lamb-lentil stew

Stuffed baked tomatoes

Dinner roll

Rhubarb crunch

Coffee or tea (decaffeinated for some)

THURSDAY

Breakfast
Sautéed fruit

Jan's overnight eggs

Bohemian kolatchen

Coffee or tea (decaffeinated for some)

Lunch
Jan's fish chowder

Coleslaw

Hard roll with butter

Fresh pear

Coffee or tea (decaffeinated for some)

Dinner
Jan's meat loaf*

Poppy seed noodles

Baked corn

Berry fruit salad

Coffee or tea (decaffeinated for some)

---

*Do not use the store's prepared meat loaf because most times it is mixed with sausage, has MSG in it, or both.

FRIDAY

Breakfast
Cranapple juice

Minute-fried steaks

Waffles sprinkled with crushed macadamia nuts and berry syrup

Coffee or tea (decaffeinated for some)

Lunch
Seafood aspic

Popovers

Apple slices in orange juice

Coffee or tea (decaffeinated for some)

Dinner
Onion soup

Baked stuffed salmon

Glorified vegetables

Wheat-rice pilaf

Ginger melon balls

Coffee or tea (decaffeinated for some)

SATURDAY

Brunch
Spiced peaches

Mushroom and egg delight over noodles

Mini parkerhouse rolls

Cinnamon coffee or tea (decaffeinated for some)

Dinner
Cold cucumber soup and bread sticks

Char-broiled steak, your favorite cut

Sautéed zucchini and onions

Restuffed baked potatoes

Strawberry shortcake with fresh strawberries

Lemon water, iced

SUNDAY

Breakfast/Brunch
Finger fruits, marinated

Shrimp-stuffed pancakes

Coffee or tea (decaffeinated for some)

Company Dinner
Wilted green salad

Chicken, fried, baked or roasted

Real mashed potatoes and onion gravy

Acorn squash cups with creamed spinach

Fresh cooked cranberries

Dinner rolls and preserves

French apple pie

Coffee or tea (decaffeinated for some)

General Recipes

7

GENERAL RECIPES

GINGER MELON BALLS

---

melons (use whatever is in season; amount depends on
how many people you plan to serve)

1 cup lemonade

crystallized ginger

Scoop out melon balls. Place them in a bowl and pour a cup of lemonade over them. Mix in a couple of pieces of crystallized ginger. Allow the mixture to marinate in the refrigerator for several hours. Before serving, remove the ginger. Serve the fruit in chilled bowls.

PEAR AND PEACH COMPOTE

---

1 16-oz can pears

1 16-oz can peaches

1 11-oz can mandarin oranges

1 t crystallized ginger (cut in slivers)

Mix all of the ingredients together, and chill a few hours before serving so that the ginger has a chance to penetrate the fruit. Remove the ginger bits before serving, as they are bitter to taste.

FRIED CINNAMON APPLES

4 green or golden delicious apples
1/2 cup unsalted butter
1/4 cup brown sugar
1/4 cup raisins
1 T cinnamon

Peel the apples. Slice them and brown them in the butter and brown sugar. Add the raisins just long enough to coat them with the sugar and the butter. Do not overcook. If you do, you will end up with applesauce. Sprinkle the cinnamon atop before serving.

For a variation on this recipe, add one large can of yams to the apples. This makes a nice side dish for four people.

FINGER FRUIT

cherries with their stems attached
grapes, cut in half
bananas, thickly sliced
orange slices
apples, quartered
apricot juice

Add the apricot juice to the fruit, using enough juice to cover the fruit. Chill. Drain off the juice before serving.

SPICED PEACHES

---

1 16-oz can cling peaches (halves)

1/4 cup honey

4 whole cloves

cinnamon-sugar

Drain syrup from peaches into a small saucepan; place peaches in a medium-size bowl. Stir honey and cloves into syrup; heat to boiling. Simmer 15 minutes, then strain over peaches. Chill—the longer the better. When ready to serve, drain peaches (being sure to remove the cloves); pour into chilled serving dishes and sprinkle with the cinnamon-sugar mixture.

SAUTÉED FRUIT

Your choice of fruit. It very much depends on the season. You may use a combination of fresh and canned.

2 T butter
1/2 cup brown sugar
1 T amaretto liqueur
peaches, sliced (about 1 cup)
cherries, halved (about 1/2 cup)
pears, sliced (about 1 cup)
apricots, sliced (about 1/2 cup)
mandarin oranges (about 1/2 cup)
apples, sliced (about 1 cup)

Melt the butter and dissolve the brown sugar in this. Add the amaretto liqueur to this, and then add the fruit and its juices. Sauté the fruit until it is coated nicely. The harmful ingredient of the amaretto should be burned out by the time the fruit passes through it. (I would still only use a very small amount and beware.) This serves 4-6 people. Serve warm.

ACORN SQUASH CUPS

2 medium-size acorn squash

1/2 cup butter

1/2 cup brown sugar

pepper to taste

Wash the squashes. Pierce the skin with a sharp fork. Place the whole squashes in the oven at 350° and bake until they begin to get soft, about 45 minutes. Remove from the oven and let cool enough to handle. Cut the squashes in half and spoon out the seeds. Butter the inside of the squash cups and sprinkle with the brown sugar and pepper. Wrap in foil paper and continue to bake them in a 350° oven for 35 more minutes.

To vary this recipe, you may spoon prepared creamed spinach or small peas into the squash cavities just before serving.

STUFFED BAKED TOMATOES

1 cup prepared, steamed wild rice
6 medium tomatoes (about 2 lb)
1 T butter
1/4 cup onion, chopped
6 t Miracle Whip salad dressing
1/4 cup fine buttered bread crumbs
6 small parsley sprigs

Heat oven to 350°. Prepare the wild rice as directed on the package, and set aside. Wash tomatoes; remove the stems and scoop out the pulp from each tomato, leaving a 1/2-inch wall. Chop the pulp to measure 1/2 cup. Mix together the wild rice, butter, pulp and chopped onion. Fill the tomatoes with the mixture. Put one level teaspoon of the salad dressing on top of each tomato. Sprinkle the fine butter crumbs on top of the salad dressing. Place the filled tomatoes in an ungreased baking dish. Bake 20-25 minutes or until heated through. Garnish with parsley. Be sure not to overcook or the tomato will become mushy and fall apart.

BAKED CORN

1/4 cup chopped onions

1/4 cup chopped green peppers

2 T unsalted butter

2 T flour

1/2 t paprika

1/4 t dry mustard

dash of pepper

3/4 cup milk

1 16-oz can whole kernel corn, drained

1 egg, slightly beaten

bread crumbs (for garnish)

Sauté the onions and peppers in the butter until golden. Blend in the flour, paprika, mustard, and pepper; cook until bubbly. Gradually add the milk. Bring to a boil. Boil for 1 minute, stirring constantly. Remove from heat. Add the corn and the egg, and pour into a 1-qt baking dish. Top with bread crumbs. Dot the top of the casserole with dabs of butter. Bake in moderate oven (350°) for 20 to 30 minutes. Yields 4-6 servings.

RE-STUFFED BAKED POTATO

6 medium-size baking potatoes
1/2 cup sour cream
1/4 cup chives
1 T bacon bits
3 T butter
1/2 t mustard
pepper to taste

Bake 6 medium baking potatoes in a 350° oven for an hour or until tender. Let the potatoes cool. Cut the potatoes in half and scoop out the insides, leaving about 1/4-inch of the potato with the skin. Leave the potato skins intact. Put the potato pulp into a bowl and mix the sour cream, chives, bacon bits (a bit of the real thing for a little taste), butter, mustard and pepper all together. Fill the potato skins with the mixture and return them to the oven for reheating and browning on top. Bake them in the 350° oven for approximately 10 minutes, or until they are steaming. You may also make these up ahead of time, wrap in foil and freeze for later use.

SHARON'S FRENCH FRIED ONION RINGS

(Walla Walla sweets are wonderful. I usually double this recipe.)

1 cup plus 2 T flour
1 egg, separated
1 cup milk
2 T vegetable oil
6 medium onions, sliced 1/4-inch thick
additional flour on plate

Beat together the 1 cup plus 2 T flour, egg yolk, milk and oil just until well moistened. Beat the egg white until soft peaks form, and fold into the flour mixture. Separately coat the onion rings with additional flour and then dip in batter. Fry a few at a time in deep fat, 375°. Stir once to separate rings. Drain on paper towels. Sprinkle lightly with pepper. May be kept in oven on low heat to keep warm until you serve. This should make 8 generous helpings. They are very good.

VEGGIE PITA BREAD FILLING

1/2 head of lettuce, shredded

1/4 onion, chopped fine

1 medium cucumber, diced

1 small green pepper, chopped

2 hard-boiled eggs, chopped

1 tomato, diced

1/2 cup mayonnaise

1/2 cup yogurt

2 T cream cheese

2 T dill

In a large bowl, mix together the lettuce, onion, cucumber, pepper, eggs and tomato. Set aside. Then mix together the mayonnaise, yogurt, cream cheese and dill. Add the creamed mixture to the vegetables and chill until you are ready to fill the pita bread and enjoy. Portions depend on how many people you plan to serve. This recipe will fill 4 rounds of pita bread.

GLORIFIED VEGETABLES

---

1 prepared recipe of white sauce (recipe in this book)

1/2 cup fresh broccoli

1/2 cup carrots, sliced

1/2 cup of small onions (pearl if they are available)

1/2 cup of new peas

1/2 cup of mushrooms, sliced

1 T lemon juice

3 T butter

salt and pepper to taste

Prepare our cookbook recipe of white sauce and set aside. Clean and slice all the above vegetables. Steam all the vegetables (except the mushrooms) for about 25 minutes or until tender. The vegetables can be steamed together. About 5 minutes before they are cooked, add the mushrooms and continue steaming for the last few minutes. Drain the moisture from the vegetables and add the lemon and butter. Salt and pepper to taste. Just before serving, pour the warmed white sauce on top.

MUSHROOM AND EGG DELIGHT ON NOODLES

4 T butter
4 green onions, sliced
8 medium mushrooms, sliced
6 eggs
pepper and salt to taste
6 oz noodles (you may use homemade or packaged)
1 recipe of the white sauce

In a frying pan, melt 2 tbsp of butter. Sauté green onions and mushrooms until lightly brown. Set aside. In another pan, again melt 2 tbsp butter and scramble the eggs. Add pepper and salt to taste. Meanwhile, cook the noodles. Prepare the white sauce according to the recipe in this cookbook, and mix with the eggs, mushroom and onion mixture. Before you are ready to serve, pour the egg mixture over the noodles.

POPPY SEED NOODLES

6 oz fettucine (homemade or packaged)
2 T butter
2 T poppy seeds
1/4 cup light cream (a maybe)
1/4 t white pepper

In small saucepan, cook the fettucine until tender. In another saucepan, melt butter and stir in poppy seeds. Add the light cream and white pepper and then add the mixture to the fettucine. This makes 4 side dish servings.

CREAMED EGG CUPS

muffin tin for 12
shortening
12 slices of fresh bacon (bacon is a maybe)
12 whole eggs
1/2 cup cream (a maybe)
salt and pepper to taste

This recipe all depends on the amount of people you plan to serve and how many egg cups you fix per person. Assuming you are preparing breakfast for six people, you would use a muffin tin for twelve. Grease the muffin tin with the shortening. Brown the slices of fresh bacon. Line the sides of each tin with a slice of bacon. Put a whole raw egg in each tin and put 1 tsp of cream on top of each egg. Salt and pepper to taste. Bake in a preheated 350° oven until the eggs are set, about 5 minutes.

DEVILED EGGS

6 hard-boiled eggs

2 T homemade mayonnaise (recipe in this cookbook)

1 t light vinegar

1/2 t salt (optional)

dash of pepper

1 t prepared mustard

1/4 t paprika

Halve the cooked eggs lengthwise. Remove yolks and mash with the rest of the ingredients. Fill the egg whites with the mixture. (Cookie shooter works great for filling the eggs.) Sprinkle the top of the eggs with the paprika.

JAN'S OVERNIGHT EGGS

8 eggs

1 pt cottage cheese

8-oz cream cheese

1 T flour

1 cup chopped mushrooms

1/4 cup chopped green onions

1 10-oz pkg frozen chopped spinach, thawed and drained

bread crumbs (for garnish)

paprika

4 T unsalted butter

In a blender, mix the eggs, cottage cheese, cream cheese and flour together. Then fold in the mushrooms, onions and spinach. Pour into a greased cake pan and top with bread crumbs and dabs of butter. Sprinkle with paprika. Bake in a 350° oven for about 45 minutes. You may prepare the dish the night before and refrigerate it. In the morning, you bake the Overnight Eggs for 45 minutes in a 350° oven.

PAT'S BLUEBERRY MUFFINS

1/4 cup butter
2 eggs
1 cup sugar
2 cups flour
2 t baking powder
1/2 cup milk
1 t imitation vanilla
2 cups fresh or frozen blueberries

Beat together the butter, eggs and sugar. Sift the flour and baking powder together and add to the first mixture, alternating with the milk. Add imitation vanilla. Drain the blueberries, and then combine them with the batter. Bake in lined muffin tins at 350° for approximately 25 minutes.

BRAN MUFFINS

1-1/2 cups whole bran cereal
1 cup sour milk
1 beaten egg
1/4 cup vegetable cooking oil
1 cup all-purpose flour
1/3 cup packed brown sugar
1/2 t baking soda
2 t baking powder
3/4 cup snipped raisins

To make sour milk, add one tablespoon of lemon juice or distilled white vinegar to one cup of milk, stir to mix, and allow to sit for 15 minutes. Combine bran cereal and milk; let stand 3 minutes until the liquid is absorbed. Stir in egg and oil; set aside. Stir together flour, brown sugar, baking powder, and baking soda; make a well in the center. Add the bran mixture, stirring just till moistened (batter will be thick). Fold in the raisins. Fill greased muffin cups and bake in 400° oven for 20-25 minutes.

BUTTER HORN ROLLS

1 cup milk
1 cup unsalted butter
2 eggs
1/2 cup sugar
1-1/2 tsp salt
4 cups flour
1 pkg yeast

Scald milk. (Do not let the scalded milk get hotter than 115 degrees; if it is too hot the heat will kill the yeast and your dough will not rise.) Add butter, eggs, sugar, salt, flour and yeast. Let rise for about 20 minutes. Divide into four parts. Roll each part as you would for pie crust, spread with butter and cut in 8 pieces as you cut a pie for serving. Roll each piece from the wide end in. Let rise another 20 minutes. Bake at 400° for 10 to 12 minutes. Brush with unsalted butter while still warm.

FRENCH BREAD THE EASY WAY

2 cups hot tap water (115 degrees)
2 pkg dry yeast (5 t)
1-1/2 T sugar
1/3 cup unsalted butter
6 cups flour (approximately)

Place the water in a large bowl. Sprinkle yeast into the water. Add the sugar and let the mixture start to work. You will notice it begin to foam. Add the butter and 2 cups of flour. Stir until it is mixed well. Add more flour, one cup at a time. Mix well. When the mixture gets too heavy to mix, put it on a floured surface and knead by hand. Work the dough until it becomes smooth, elastic and nonsticky. It will take about 8 to 18 minutes to get it just right. Place the dough on a floured cloth and cover with a bowl you have greased with a solid shortening. Let dough rise in a draft-free space for about 20 minutes. Punch this down and let it rise again. Divide the dough in two equal pieces, shape and place into shortening-greased bread pans. Let the dough rise again. Bake in preheated oven of 375° for about 35 minutes. When the bread sounds hollow when tapped and is brown on top, it is done. Brush with butter.

STUFFED FRENCH TOAST

4 eggs, beaten
3 T of half and half
2 T of cooking oil
4 slices of whole wheat or white bread
1/4 cup of chopped onions, sautéed
1/4 cup of chopped green pepper, sautéed
1/2 cup of diced potatoes, fried
2 T butter
6 eggs, beaten
salt and pepper to taste

In a wide, shallow bowl, beat the first four eggs and 3 T of half and half. Set aside. Heat your skillet or frying pan to medium temperature. Add your cooking oil. Coat the slices of bread in the prepared egg mixture one at a time. Do not leave the bread sitting too long in the mixture or the bread will get too soggy and possibly fall apart. Transfer the bread to the hot skillet and brown on each side. Follow this procedure for the other slices of bread. Keep warmed while preparing the stuffing.

In another skillet, sauté the chopped onions, green pepper and diced potatoes in the butter. Let these brown for a few minutes. Add salt and pepper to taste. In a small bowl, beat the remaining six eggs and fold into the sautéed vegetables. Spoon the sautéed egg mixture between the slices of french toast, and cut in triangles. It is fine to let the egg mixture ooze out the sides of the french toast. You might like to serve this with melons and strawberries. Sprinkle a little powdered sugar on top.

BOHEMIAN KOLATCHEN

1 pkg active dry yeast
1/4 cup water
3 cups all-purpose flour
1/2 t salt
1/2 cup unsalted butter
2 eggs, beaten
1 cup yogurt
1 t imitation vanilla
1 cup prunes
3/4 cup dried apricots
1/2 cup sugar
1 T lemon juice
1/4 cup powdered sugar

Sprinkle one package of active dry yeast over 1/4 cup 110-115° water. Set aside. Sift together the all-purpose flour and the salt. Cut in the unsalted butter. Blend in yeast and add the beaten eggs, yogurt and imitation vanilla. Roll the dough into 2" balls and place on a greased baking sheet about 2" apart. Now prepare the filling. Simmer the prunes and dried apricots in water and cook until tender; drain and puree in blender or food processor with the sugar and lemon juice. Press an indentation into the center of each roll, leaving a 1/4" rim. Fill with the date mixture, cover and let rise about 40 minutes. Heat to 375°. Bake approximately 20 minutes and sprinkle with powdered sugar while still warm.

NEVER-FAIL PANCAKES

1 egg
1-1/4 cup sour milk (Add 4 t vinegar to 1-1/4 cups milk and let stand 15 minutes.)
2 T cooking oil
1 cup of all-purpose flour
1 T sugar
2 t baking powder

Mix the above ingredients until slightly lumpy. Lightly grease a heavy skillet and heat until water sprinkled on the skillet dances across the surface. Pour about 1/4 cup of batter on skillet for each pancake.

CREAMED SALMON ON TOAST

---

1 pound of baked or cooked salmon

2 T butter

buttered and toasted bread crumbs

1 can condensed cream of mushroom soup

2 t catsup

1 T Worcestershire sauce

Pinch cayenne pepper

1/2 t salt

In a glass baking dish, alternate the salmon, butter and bread crumbs. In a small bowl, mix the cream of mushroom soup with the catsup, worcestershire, cayenne, and salt. Pour over the ingredients in the baking dish. Top with more bread crumbs, and bake in a 350° oven for 20 minutes. Serve on toast or eat as is.

POTATO YOGURT PANCAKES

6 medium-size potatoes
2 eggs, beaten
1 cup plain yogurt
1 cup flour
1 t salt
1 t sugar
1-1/2 t baking powder

Grate raw potatoes. Add the beaten eggs, yogurt and flour with salt, sugar and baking powder. Beat slightly to blend. Cook on a hot buttered griddle until nicely browned.

MINI PARKERHOUSE ROLLS

3-1/2 cups all-purpose flour
1 pkg active dry yeast
1-1/4 cups milk
1/2 cup sugar
1 egg, beaten
1/4 cup soft butter

Combine 1-1/2 cups of flour with yeast. Heat milk, sugar, beaten egg and butter until mixture is warm and everything is blended. Add to the flour mixture. Beat with your mixer or knead with your hands until well-mixed. (I use my food processor with the plastic dough blade attachment.) Mix just until smooth. Add the remaining 2 cups of flour until dough is no longer sticky when touched. It should have an elastic consistency. (If you are kneading this by hand it should take about 8 to 10 minutes.) Shape dough into a ball. Grease a large bowl and sprinkle some flour on a kitchen towel. Place the dough ball on the floured towel and place the bowl over the dough. With this air-tight method your dough should rise in 20 minutes. After this time punch your dough down and let it rise for another 20 minutes. Grease two baking sheets. Divide the dough into two balls. On a floured surface roll out each half of dough to 1/4-inch thickness. Cut with floured 1-1/2" round cookie cutter. Brush this with melted butter. Fold each circle so one half will overlap slightly. Place 1-1/2" apart on baking sheet. Cover with a clean cloth and let rise for about 35 minutes. Bake in a 375° oven for about 10 minutes.

PITA POCKET BREAD

---

1 pkg dry yeast

1-1/4 cups warm water (110-115°)

3-1/4 to 3-3/4 cups all-purpose flour

1/4 cup Crisco shortening

In a large mixing bowl, soften the yeast in the warm water. Add two cups of the flour to the shortening, and beat at low speed of an electric mixer for 1 minute. Then beat on high for 3 minutes. Stir in as much of the remaining flour as you can mix in with a spoon. Turn out onto lightly floured surface. Knead in enough of the remaining flour to make a moderately soft dough that is smooth and elastic (about 5 minutes). Cover and let rise in a warm place for 15 minutes. Divide into 12 equal portions. Roll each into a ball between floured hands. Cover with a damp warm cloth and let rest 10 minutes. Gently flatten balls without creasing dough. Work with enough flour so dough does not stick. Roll one piece of dough at a time into a 6" round, turning the dough over once, being careful not to stretch or puncture the dough. Place a couple of rounds at a time on a baking sheet and bake at 450° for about 3 minutes or until dough is puffed and softly set. Turn over with spatula and bake 2 more minutes until dough has browned lightly.

POPOVERS

1-1/2 t shortening
2 eggs, beaten
1 cup milk
1 T cooking oil
1 cup all-purpose flour
dash salt

Preheat oven to 450°. Grease six 6-oz custard cups with 1/4 t of the shortening for each cup. Place custard cups on a 15 by 10 by 1 inch baking pan or sheet and place in oven. Meanwhile, in mixing bowl, combine beaten eggs, milk and oil. Add flour and salt. Beat with mixer until smooth. Fill the hot custard cups half full. Bake in 450° oven for 20 minutes or until the popovers are firm. Reduce oven temperature to 350° and bake 15 more minutes. Prick each popover to let the steam escape. Serve hot.

POTATO BREAD

2 pkg yeast
1 cup warm water (use potato water)
2 T sugar
1/2 cup shortening
2 medium potatoes, boiled and mashed smooth
1 cup milk
5 to 7 cups flour

Soften yeast in potato water with sugar. Add shortening, potatoes, milk and 1 cup flour. Mix until smooth. Add more flour one cup at a time, beating mixture after each cup. When dough gets too stiff, put it on a floured surface and knead by hand. Knead the dough until it gets smooth and elastic. Dough may be placed on a floured surface and covered with a shortening-greased bowl to rise. Let your dough rise twice. It should take about 20 minutes to rise each time. Divide dough into two parts. Place them in shortening-greased bread pans and let rise for the last time. Bake bread in 375° oven for 35 minutes or until loaves sound hollow when tapped. Remove them from their pans when done and cool on a wire rack.

Tips on your potato bread: If using the Kitchen Aid mixer and its dough hook, mix for approximately 10 minutes. When dough leaves the hook, add flour. Never use more flour than the recipe calls for. When you think you have enough flour, wash your hands and put your fingers in the dough. If the dough comes out sticky, it needs more flour. If not, then let rise.

POTATO ROLLS

---

1 cup mashed potatoes (real potatoes, not instant)

1 cup lukewarm water

1 cup sugar

1 pkg yeast

1 cup melted butter

4 eggs, well beaten

approximately 6-1/4 cups flour

powdered sugar to garnish

Mix the potatoes, water, sugar and yeast. Let rise in a warm place overnight. In the morning, add the melted butter, eggs and enough flour to make a very soft dough. Form the rolls into balls the size of a walnut by rolling the dough in your hands. Keep your hands well buttered and this will prevent them from being sticky. Place the rolls close together on a greased baking pan and then let rise until double in size. Bake in a 400° oven for approximately 12 minutes, until they are nice and brown. Melt 4 T of butter over the top when they are finished and then sprinkle with powdered sugar. They are almost like sweet rolls.

STICKY BUNS

1/2 cup light corn syrup

1/3 cup packed brown sugar

3 T unsalted butter

1 T water

2 cups all-purpose flour

1 T baking powder

1/3 cup shortening

3/4 cup milk

1/4 cup granulated sugar

1/2 t ground cinnamon

In a saucepan, combine syrup, brown sugar, butter and water. Cook and stir over low heat until brown sugar is dissolved. Do not boil or the mixture will caramelize and you do not want this consistency. Spread on the bottom of a 9 by 9 by 2 baking pan.

In a mixing bowl, stir together flour and baking powder. Cut in shortening until crumbly and make a well in the center. Add the milk and stir until the dough clings together. Turn the dough out onto a floured surface and knead gently for 20 strokes. Roll out into a rectangle. Combine sugar and cinnamon; sprinkle over dough. Roll up, beginning with long side. Slice into 1″ slices. Place cut side down in prepared pan. Bake in 425° oven for 30 minutes or until brown. Loosen side and immediately invert on serving plate. This recipe should make 12 buns.

WHOLE WHEAT BREAD

3 cups whole wheat flour
2 pkg dry yeast
1 t salt
3 cups water
1/2 cup honey
2 T liquid Crisco (oil)
1 cup whole wheat flour
1 cup wheat germ or bran (optional)
4 – 4-1/2 cups white flour

Combine the 3 cups whole wheat flour, dry yeast, and salt in a large mixing bowl. Set aside. Heat the water, honey and Crisco in a saucepan over low heat. When liquid is warm, not hot, mix the liquid into the dry ingredients with an electric mixer at low speed. With a spoon, blend in one more cup of whole wheat flour and, if you desire, add one cup of wheat germ or bran. Now add 4 - 4-1/2 cups of white flour. Mix and knead for about 5 minutes. Place dough in a bowl which has been greased with solid shortening, and cover with wax paper and cloth. Place in a warm, draft-free place, and let rise for an hour. Knead again for a few minutes; divide into 3 portions. Place in greased loaf baking dishes. Let rise another 45 minutes. Bake for 35 to 40 minutes in a 350° oven.

WHOLE WHEAT MUFFINS

---

1 egg, beaten slightly with fork

1 cup milk

1/4 cup salad oil or melted shortening

1/2 cup flour

1/3 cup sugar

2 t baking powder

1 t salt

1/2 cup bran

1 cup whole wheat flour

1/2 cup raisins (optional)

Mix together the egg, milk, and salad oil. Combine the flour, sugar, baking powder, salt, bran and whole wheat flour with the egg mixture. Stir just until moistened; do not overmix. (Batter should be lumpy.) Add raisins if desired. Fill greased muffin cups 2/3 full. Bake at 400° for 20-25 minutes.

NEVER-FAIL WAFFLES

2 cups flour
2-1/2 t baking powder
1 t sugar
2 egg yolks—reserve egg whites
6 T melted butter
1-1/4 cups milk
1 t sugar

Sift together the flour, baking powder, and sugar. Add the egg yolks, butter, milk and sugar. Fold in the 2 reserved egg whites, beaten stiff. Cook the waffles, following the cooking time recommended for your waffle iron.

YEAST BAGELS

4-1/2 cups all-purpose flour

2 pkg active dry yeast

1-1/2 cups warm water (110° to 115°)

3 T sugar

1 egg

1/4 t salt

2 T sugar

In a mixing bowl, combine 1-1/2 cups of flour and the yeast. Combine the warm water, the 3 T of sugar and the egg. Pour over flour mixture. Add the salt last. (Salt, if added too soon, will kill the yeast.) Beat at low speed on your mixer for one minute. Now beat at high speed for 3 minutes. Mix in the remaining flour with your hands. Turn onto a floured board and continue kneading the dough until stiff, smooth and elastic, about 8 minutes. (If you have a food processor you may use this to knead your dough. You use your plastic dough blade with the processor, and mix until dough is no longer sticky when touched.) Cover and let dough rise 20 minutes in a draft-free place. Divide the dough into 12 portions. Shape each portion into a ball and punch a hole in the center of each. Place on a greased baking sheet and let rise for 20 more minutes. Broil 5 minutes to set the bagels, turning after 2-1/2 minutes. Do not let them brown. Bring a gallon of water to boiling and add the remaining 2 T of sugar to this. Drop the bagels into the boiling water and let cook for seven minutes, turning once. Drain. Place on greased baking sheet and bake at 375° for 25 to 30 minutes. This should yield a dozen bagels.

WALLA WALLA GREEN SALAD

1 large head bibb lettuce
1 medium or large can mandarin oranges
2 sliced avocados
1 medium-size Walla Walla onion, sliced (can substitute any sweet yellow onion if Walla Wallas are unavailable)

Mix all of the ingredients together and add to your bibb lettuce. Then pour over this your own French dressing or a regular bottled French dressing, preferably low-calorie. Chill a few minutes before you are ready to serve this and it is wonderful.

CABBAGE SALAD

2 cups regular vinegar
2 cups sugar
2 T mustard seed
2 T celery seed
1 large head of cabbage
6 small green onions
2 green peppers
2 carrots

Heat the vinegar, sugar, mustard seed and celery seed until the sugar melts. Cool and then chop the cabbage, onions, peppers and carrots. Mix all the ingredients together and chill. This is ready to serve as soon as it is cold. It may be stored in the refrigerator for up to a week.

CUCUMBER SALAD

1 6-oz pkg lime jello
2 cups boiling water
1/2 t salt (maybe)
3 T regular vinegar
2 slices of onion, diced
1 cup sour cream (this is a maybe)
1/2 cup mayonnaise
1 medium-size cucumber, peeled and chopped

Dissolve the lime jello in the boiling water. Add the salt (if using), the vinegar, and the diced onion. Chill until slightly thickened. Fold in the sour cream and mayonnaise. Blend thoroughly. Fold the cucumber into the mixture. Chill until firm.

VANILLA PUDDING SALAD

---

1 small pkg orange jello

1 small pkg vanilla pudding

2-1/2 cups water and juice from mandarin oranges

1 pkg Dream Whip, prepared as directed on pkg

1 can mandarin oranges, drained (reserve the juice)

3 to 4 sliced bananas

In a saucepan, combine the orange jello mix, vanilla pudding mix, water and juice from the mandarin oranges. Bring this to a boil and cool. Prepare a package of the Dream Whip according to the directions on the box, and fold this into the pudding mixture. Add the mandarin oranges and the sliced bananas. Pour this into a bowl and refrigerate for at least two hours, allowing it to thicken.

LOW-CALORIE POTATO SALAD

2 T plain vinegar
2 green onions, chopped
2 T water
2 cups diced, cooked potatoes
1 cup diced celery
1/2 cup diced red and green peppers, mixed
2 hard-cooked egg whites
1/4 cup plain yogurt
2 T low-calorie french dressing

Mix the first two ingredients with 2 T water. Blend thoroughly. Pour mixture over potatoes and refrigerate until potatoes are chilled. Mix in celery, peppers and chopped egg white. Combine yogurt and dressing and add to the potatoes, mixing well. Season to taste. Serve on salad greens. This should make about eight 1/2-cup servings. Contains 35 calories per 1/2 cup.

TUNA CANTALOUPE RING SALAD

1 large cantaloupe
4 lettuce leaves, cleaned
1 can water-packed tuna
2 T Miracle Whip salad dressing
1 t curry powder
1 T lemon juice
1/2 cup seedless green grapes
1/2 cup mandarin oranges, drained
1 sprig mint
1 T french dressing

Cut the cantaloupe crosswise into six slices. Take out the seeds, rinse and peel. Place the cantaloupe in a ring on top of salad greens. Set aside. Mix together the tuna, Miracle Whip salad dressing, curry powder and lemon juice. Scoop this mixture in the middle of the cantaloupe ring. Garnish with green grapes, mandarin oranges and a mint sprig. One tablespoon of french dressing is a nice finishing touch on top of the salad.

TOMATO ASPIC WITH VEGETABLES "A GOOD OL' SOUTHERN RECIPE"

3 cups canned tomato juice

3 ribs celery, diced

1 small onion, sliced

2 lemon slices

2 t chili sauce

1 small bay leaf

1 t salt, depending on your overload

2-1/2 envelopes unflavored gelatin

2/3 cup cold tomato juice

1/4 cup cider vinegar

1 cup finely shredded cabbage

1/4 cup chopped celery

1/4 cup shredded carrots

1/4 cup chopped cucumbers

6 chopped green onions

Combine 3 cups tomato juice with celery, onion slices, lemon slices, chili sauce, bay leaf and salt. Simmer 10 minutes. Strain. Meanwhile, sprinkle gelatin over 2/3 cup of tomato juice and vinegar in bowl. When softened, stir in hot tomato juice mixture and stir until gelatin is dissolved. Refrigerate, stirring occasionally until mixture thickens, about 1-2 hours. Fold vegetables into the gelatin mixture. Pour into individual molds or one large mold and refrigerate until firm. You may also add seafood like crab and shrimp. Good atop lettuce leaves.

SEAFOOD ASPIC

---

3 cups tomato juice

1 t salt

1 t sugar

1 t lemon juice

1 t Worcestershire sauce

1 very small onion, finely diced

dash of Tabasco

2 envelopes unflavored gelatin

1/2 cup cold water

1 avocado, chopped

1/2 cup celery, chopped fine

1 cup cleaned and drained crab meat

1 cup small shrimp, cleaned and drained

Boil the tomato juice with the seasonings. Steep 10 to 15 minutes. Add gelatin that has been softened in cold water. Stir until the gelatin has melted. Cool until the mixture begins to thicken. Prepare the seafood. Add the seafood to the aspic after it has thickened, and pour into the mold. Garnish the aspic with the avocado and celery, topped with a dab of mayonnaise.

CHICKEN-FILLED CREPES

Basic Crepe

1 cup all-purpose flour
1-1/2 cups milk
2 eggs
1 T cooking oil

In a mixing bowl, combine the above ingredients with a mixer. Heat a lightly greased skillet. (I like to use the electric inverted crepe pan. If you do not have one, you may use a 6″ skillet.) Remove from heat; spoon in about 2 T of batter. Return to heat and brown one side only. Remove crepe by placing inverted pan over a paper towel. This recipe makes approximately 18.

Chicken Filling

6 T butter
pepper to taste
garlic to taste
6 T all-purpose flour
3 cups milk
1/2 cup fresh sliced mushrooms
1 10-oz pkg chopped broccoli
2 cups finely chopped cooked chicken
12 basic main-dish crepes

Melt butter. Blend in the flour and add the milk. Cook, stirring constantly until thick. Set 1/2 cup of sauce aside and then add the fresh mushrooms. Cook the broccoli according to the package directions; drain. Combine the drained broccoli, chicken and the 1/2 cup of reserved sauce. Spread 1/4 cup of filling over the unbrowned side of the crepe, leaving a 1/2″ rim around the edge. Roll up the crepe. Place the seam side down in the skillet or chafing dish. Drizzle the sauce over the crepes.

CHINESE CHICKEN SALAD

1 or 2 chicken breasts
1 bundle or 2 oz Chinese long rice (cellophane noodles)
1 head lettuce, shredded
4 stalks of green onion, chopped
2 T toasted sesame seeds
1/2 cup sliced fresh mushrooms
2 T sugar
1/2 t salt
1/2 t pepper
1/4 cup salad oil
3 T white vinegar
1 T sesame oil

Cook the chicken breasts by boiling them in water with a little salt. Cool and shred them. Deep-fry the long rice until it expands. Combine the chicken and rice with the lettuce, onion, sesame seeds and mushrooms. Refrigerate.

Combine the sugar, salt, pepper, salad oil, vinegar and sesame oil in a jar. Shake well. Refrigerate. When you are ready to serve, add the dressing to the salad and toss lightly. Serve immediately.

CHICKEN AND DUMPLINGS

Chicken

1 whole chicken
3 qts boiling water
1 medium onion, chopped
2 medium carrots, shredded
2 stalks celery, chopped
salt to taste (depending on your salt load)
pepper to taste

Boil the above ingredients until the chicken falls off the bone. Remove the bone from the stock.

Dumplings

1 egg, beaten
1 cup milk
3 T melted butter
3 t baking soda
1-2 cups flour (Gradually add flour until the batter becomes stiff. You may not use all of the 2 cups.)

Mix the above ingredients and drop by spoonfuls on top of chicken. Steam for 15 to 20 minutes over low heat. Be sure not to take the lid off the kettle while cooking.

PAT'S CURRIED CHICKEN

Chicken

1/4 cup flour
1/4 t pepper
2-1/2 to 3 lbs of chicken breasts and thighs
1 T butter or margarine
curry sauce (recipe follows)

Mix flour and pepper; dredge chicken parts in mixture. Place skin side up in a baking dish, and dot with butter. Preheat oven to 450° and bake chicken till well browned, 20 to 30 minutes.

While the chicken bakes, make the curry sauce.

Curry Sauce

1/4 cup finely minced onion
1 T curry powder
1 T tomato paste
1/4 cup lemon juice (juice of 1 large lemon)
1 cup chicken broth
1 clove garlic, crushed

Mix all ingredients together in a small saucepan and heat over medium heat; stir to combine well. Cook for 10 minutes. When chicken is browned, cover with sauce. Reduce oven to 350° and bake for another 10 to 15 minutes. Remove to platter and serve with rice pilaf.

SWEET-AND-SOUR CHICKEN

2 lbs chicken wings

2 eggs, beaten

1/2 cup corn starch

2 T oil

1 whole garlic clove, minced

scant salt

pepper to taste

1/2 cup sugar

1 t cornstarch

1/2 cup white vinegar

1/4 cup chicken bouillon or stock

3 T ketchup

Clean the chicken wings. Dip the chicken into the beaten eggs and roll in the cornstarch; fry in oil and minced garlic until brown. Arrange the chicken in a baking pan, and sprinkle with the scant salt and the pepper. Set aside. In a saucepan, combine the sugar and 1 t of cornstarch. Stir in the vinegar, chicken stock and ketchup. Cook at a low temperature until this begins to thicken. Pour over the browned chicken wings and bake in a 350° oven for 1/2 hour. After the first 10 minutes in the oven, turn the chicken over. This will allow all sides of the chicken to become coated with the sauce. You may also try this with shrimp. Serve with rice.

CHICKEN BROCCOLI CASSEROLE

---

2 10-oz pkgs frozen broccoli. (You may use fresh broccoli but it is easier to use frozen.)

---

2 lbs chicken breasts, cooked.

---

1 cup of light cream (a maybe)

1/2 cup sour cream

---

1 cup mayonnaise

---

1 t lemon juice

1/2 t curry powder

1/2 cup ricotta cheese

3/4 cup soft bread crumbs

---

1 T unsalted butter

When you have cooked your chicken breasts, I am assuming that you have boiled them. I would like you to reserve 1 cup of broth that you have cooked the chicken breasts in, and then add 1 cup of light cream.

Butter the casserole dish. Boil broccoli until tender. Put this in the dish along with the chicken. The chicken breasts should be cut up into bite-size pieces. Combine chicken broth, cream, mayonnaise, lemon juice, curry powder, sour cream, ricotta cheese and one-half of the bread crumbs. Pour this over the chicken and broccoli. Then sprinkle the remaining 1/4 cup of bread crumbs over the entire casserole, dabbing with unsalted butter. Bake this, uncovered, at 350° for 30 minutes, until it is heated through. This should serve about 6 people generously.

BEEF KABOBS

1 cup vegetable oil
1/4 cup lemon juice
1 bay leaf
1/2 t oregano
1/4 t pepper
3 lbs lean beef cut in 1″ cubes
4 small onions cut in 1/4″ slices
1 basket cherry tomatoes
2 green peppers, seeded and quartered

Combine the oil, lemon juice, bay leaf, oregano and pepper. Pour the marinade over the meat and refrigerate for several hours. Thread the skewers and broil, basting with the leftover marinade. Wonderful when served on a bed of rice.

BAKED STUFFED COD WITH CREAMED SHRIMP SAUCE

1 6-8 lb cod fish
2 cups dry bread crumbs
1 cup raw mushrooms, chopped
1/2 cup fresh parsley, chopped
1/2 cup unsalted melted butter
1/4 t marjoram
1 cup raw carrots, finely grated
3/4 cup onions, finely chopped, sautéed in butter
1 egg
1 pepper, chopped

Combine all the above ingredients except codfish; mix well. Pack lightly in the cavity of a cleaned, preferably fresh, cod fish, weighing approximately 6 to 8 pounds. (Have your butcher prepare your fish for stuffing. He will know what to do.) Heat your oven to 350°; place fish on aluminum foil in a baking dish or bake in an open barbecue pot. Bake 20 minutes per pound, about 2 hours.

For the shrimp sauce, use our basic white sauce recipe and add fresh cooked shrimp to this.

LAMB-LENTIL STEW

8 cups water
2 cups red lentils
3 large cloves garlic
4 T unsalted butter
4 T Crisco oil
2 large onions, chopped
3 lbs lamb stew meat, cut in 1" pieces
1 T sugar
4 large tomatoes, peeled and pureed
1/2 t white pepper
1-1/2 lbs fresh green beans
1/4 t ground cumin (optional)
yogurt

Pour the 8 cups of water into a soup kettle and add the lentils and garlic. Simmer for about 1-1/2 hours to tenderize the lentils. Heat the butter and the oil in a heavy skillet. Peel and chop the onions and sauté slowly until golden brown. Brown the lamb pieces with the onion. Stir in the sugar and pureed tomatoes, and add to the lentil soup kettle. Add the white pepper. Cover and simmer for 45 minutes. When meat is tender, add green beans. Sprinkle with the ground cumin. Cook over low heat until beans are tender. 5 minutes before serving, add a cup of yogurt to thicken the stew. Serve hot with melba toast. An unusual Middle Eastern treat.

LASAGNA

---

1 lb hamburger, preferably ground round

1 T whole basil leaf

1 T oregano

2 cups tomatoes

2 6-oz cans tomato paste

1/2 cup chopped onion

garlic to taste

10 oz lasagna noodles

1 lb cottage cheese (this is a maybe)

1 cup ricotta cheese (this is a maybe) or cheese substitute

2 T parsley flakes

1 beaten egg

1/2 T pepper

Brown the meat slowly and spoon off the fat. Add the basil leaves, oregano, tomatoes, tomato paste, onions and garlic. Simmer this for 30 minutes. While this is simmering, cook the lasagna noodles in a large amount of water, until they are tender. Drain them and rinse the starch off the noodles. Then combine the cottage cheese and ricotta cheese (again, these are a maybe on our diet), parsley flakes, beaten egg and pepper. Place one half of the noodles in a greased 13 by 9 by 2 inch cake pan or baking dish. Spread your first layer of noodles with one half of the cottage cheese filling and if by this time you have found a cheese substitute (they say one is to be on the market soon), then you may add the cheese substitute over the next layer or on top of the cottage cheese filling. (If you do not have a cheese substitute and if you do not know which cheeses you can tolerate and which you cannot, then leave the cheese out. If ricotta cheese is all right for your diet, then you can use that instead.) Add, after the cottage cheese, one half of the meat mixture, and repeat the layers. You should end up with a little tomato sauce on the top layer of your noodles so that the noodles do not stick to the cover of the casserole dish or to the tin foil that you may use to cover this. Bake this at 375° for 30 to 45 minutes. We suggest that you bake this covered. Let the lasagna stand for approximately 10 minutes before cutting, so that it has a chance to settle. You will find that even though there is no mozzarella cheese on top of this lasagna, it still tastes very good.

BAKED MAHI-MAHI

mahi-mahi (can be found in specialty grocery stores)
2 T butter
paprika

Brown the mahi-mahi in 2 T butter. Place in baking dish and sprinkle with paprika. Bake for 15 minutes, turning in the pan once.

LIVER AND ONIONS OVER TOAST

1/2 cup flour
salt and pepper to taste
1 lb calf's liver
1/2 cup vegetable oil
1 cup water
2 cups milk
3 medium-size sweet onions, sliced thin
1/2 cup diced green pepper (optional)
1 cup sliced mushrooms (optional)
3 T butter
1 T garlic powder

Flour, salt and pepper a pound of calf's liver and brown it in 1/2 cup of vegetable oil. Add the water and milk to the liver. Simmer. Gradually the liquid will begin thickening, making its own gravy. Stir this occasionally. If it gets too thick, you may wish to add a little more milk. In another skillet, over low heat, brown the sliced onions, pepper and mushrooms in the butter. Add these vegetables to the liver and gravy. Sprinkle in the garlic powder. Cover and simmer until the liver is tender to your liking, watching carefully so that it does not overcook. Check the seasonings once again for enough salt and pepper. This recipe should not take you longer than 30-45 minutes to prepare. You then serve it hot over toast points or mashed potatoes.

CURRIED MEATBALLS

1 16-oz can tomatoes
3/4 cup soft bread crumbs
1-1/2 lb ground beef
1/4 cup chopped onions
scant salt
1/8 t pepper
1/4 cup flour
3 T lard or Crisco
1/2 t sugar
1/2 t curry powder
1/4 t pepper
4 cups hot, cooked rice

Drain 1/2 cup juice from tomatoes. Reserve remaining juice and tomatoes. Pour 1/2 cup tomato juice over the bread crumbs. Add beef, onion, salt and pepper. Mix thoroughly. Shape mixture into 24 balls, using one rounded tablespoon for each. Dredge meatballs in flour. Brown in Crisco. Pour off the drippings. Add the remaining tomatoes and juice, sugar, curry powder and pepper. Cook slowly for 20 minutes. Serve this over rice. Should serve 6 to 8 people.

JAN'S MEAT LOAF

Meat Loaf

2 lb lean ground beef
1 medium onion, chopped
1 egg
fresh ground pepper to taste
1/4 cup catsup
1 cup buttered bread crumbs

Sauce

1/2 cup catsup
1/4 cup brown sugar
1 T white vinegar
1/4 t nutmeg
1 T mustard

Mix the meat loaf ingredients. Set aside. Mix together the sauce ingredients. Pour the sauce over the meat loaf. Bake in a 350° oven for 45 minutes or until done.

PORK-VEGETABLE BAKE

1-1/2 lbs pork tenderloin

1/2 cup yellow cornmeal

1/2 cup all-purpose flour

1 T sugar

1-1/2 t baking powder

1 beaten egg

1-1/2 cups half and half

4 T corn oil

1/2 cup chopped carrots

1/4 cup chopped onion

1/4 cup chopped green pepper

1/4 cup chopped celery

1/3 cup milk

1/2 t prepared mustard

1/4 cup juice from baked pork tenderloin

Place the pork tenderloin in a covered baking dish with 1/2 cup water. Bake at 350° until tender, about an hour. While the pork is baking, stir together cornmeal, flour, sugar, and baking powder. In a separate bowl, combine egg, half and half and 2 T of the corn oil. Add to the dry ingredients; beat until smooth. Set aside. In saucepan heat remaining 2 T oil; add vegetables. Cook, covered, for 10 minutes. Blend in milk, mustard and juice from baked tenderloin. Stir in the pork tenderloin (cut in bite-size pieces). After this has cooked together for a couple of minutes, turn it into a greased casserole dish. Spoon batter atop hot mixture and bake uncovered at 400° for 25 minutes. Serves 4.

STUFFED FRESH PORK
OR VEAL CHOPS

1/2 cup chopped onion

1/2 cup sliced fresh mushrooms

1/4 cup diced celery

1 t ground sage

1/4 t pepper

8 cups dry bread crumbs

1 cup chicken broth (preferably homemade)

4 pork or veal chops prepared for stuffing. Ask the butcher to cut them at least 1-1/2" thick and sliced for stuffing.

Mix the onion, mushrooms, celery, sage, pepper, bread crumbs and chicken broth. You may find you need a little more liquid if the mixture is too dry. If you do, just add milk or warm water. Stuff the filling in the cavity of the pork or veal chop. (Remember, fresh pork is a maybe, so be aware of this and do not overindulge.) Bake, covered, at 350° for approximately 1 hour.

POTATO BURGERS

2 eggs, beaten
1 small onion, minced
2 slices of bread, shredded
2 medium-size potatoes
1/2 lb ground beef
3 T ketchup
scant salt
dash pepper
2 T cornstarch

Beat the eggs and add minced onion and bread. Peel and grate the potatoes into egg mixture. Mix immediately to prevent potatoes from discoloring. Add ground beef and seasonings. Sprinkle the cornstarch on top and mix well. Heat a pan with oil. Drop by spoonfuls and cook over medium heat with the cover on. Brown on both sides.

BAKED STUFFED SALMON

1 6-lb salmon (Have your butcher clean this specially for stuffing.)
1 lb crab meat, cooked
4 cups bread crumbs
1/4 cup chopped onion
2 T parsley
1/2 cup butter
crushed pepper to taste

Combine crab meat and remaining ingredients. Stuff salmon with mixture until completely full. Wrap the entire fish in foil and bake at 350° for 2 hours, or about 20 minutes per pound.

SALMON CASSEROLE

10 oz canned salmon
2 T chopped onion
4 T butter
3 T flour
2 T horseradish
scant salt
1/4 t pepper
1 can evaporated milk
2 cups cooked noodles
1 cup cooked peas or whole kernel corn

Drain and flake the salmon, reserving the liquid. Measure the salmon liquid and add enough water to make 1 cup. Cook onion in butter until tender but not brown. Remove from heat and blend in the flour and seasonings. Gradually add the milk, mixing this until smooth. Add the salmon liquid/water mixture and blend well. Cook over low heat, stirring until thickened and smooth. Arrange alternate layers of salmon, noodles and peas or corn in a greased 1-1/2 qt casserole. Pour sauce over top. Bake in 400° oven for 25 to 30 minutes or until top bubbles and is lightly browned.

SALMON TOFU LOAF

---

2 eggs, beaten

3/4 cup evaporated milk

1 can mushroom soup (maybe)

2 T oil or melted margarine

1/2 cup bread crumbs

1/2 can salmon (15-1/2 oz)

1/2 cup chopped onions

1 large carrot, grated

1 block of tofu, well drained and cubed

1/4 cup sliced green onions

parsley flakes

Beat the eggs and add milk, mushroom soup, oil, bread crumbs, salmon, chopped onions and grated carrot. Mix this all well and add tofu cubes. Mix well, garnish with parsley flakes and sliced onions, and bake in a greased loaf pan at 350° to 375° for approximately 1 hour.

SHRIMP GUMBO

3 lbs shrimp
4 T oil
2 T flour
3 cups okra, chopped
2 onions, chopped
1 can tomatoes
2 qts water
1 bay leaf
3 cloves garlic
scant salt
1/4 t pepper

Boil the shrimp for three minutes. Peel and devein the cooked shrimp. Heat 2 T of the oil and brown the flour. Add the shrimp to this for a few minutes, stirring constantly. Set it aside. Brown the okra and onions in the remaining 2 T oil. Add tomatoes when the okra is nearly cooked. Add water, bay leaf, garlic, salt and pepper. Add shrimp and browned flour mixture to this. Cover and cook slowly for 30 minutes. Serve on a bed of rice.

JAN'S FISH CHOWDER

---

1 8-oz can tomato paste

---

1 can Ro-tel tomatoes (this brand is essential because it is spicy

---

1 large can stewed tomatoes

---

1 8-oz can tomato sauce

---

1 large onion, sliced

---

1 bunch of green onions, diced, including tops

---

1 green pepper, seeded and chopped

---

2 large cloves of garlic (leave these whole so they may be taken out before serving. You may put a toothpick through them so they will be easily identified.)

1/3 cup parsley, chopped (for the best taste, use fresh parsley)

1/3 cup olive oil (if this is a maybe for you, I suggest using salad oil)

---

8 oz white wine

---

4 cups water

---

2 bay leaves

---

3 t salt

---

1 t black pepper

1/2 t rosemary

1/4 t thyme

---

your choice of seafood (shrimp, cod, crab, etc.)

Heat the tomato paste, the Ro-tel tomatoes, the stewed tomatoes, and the tomato sauce in a large stew pot until simmering. Sauté the onions, pepper and spices in the oil. Add the wine and water. Now add these ingredients to the tomato base in the stew pot, and continue to simmer for about 3 hours.

(Actually, the longer it simmers, the thicker and better it will taste. As the 3 hours pass, I taste and sometimes add a little more wine and spices. Add to suit your taste.)

About 1/2 hour before you are ready to serve, add your choice of seafood. (I use shrimp, crab meat, white fish (cod), cleaned and steamed clams, and mussels. I precook the fish and add to the stew. It is good to remember not to add the fish until you are almost ready to serve it (about 30 min.) or the fish will become too rubbery. I serve the chowder with a green salad and french bread.) This is out of this world!

SHRIMP-STUFFED PANCAKES

12 oz cooked shrimp
1 small onion, chopped
1 10-oz pkg frozen chopped broccoli (thaw for recipe)
1/2 cup water
white sauce (use our recipe)
pancakes (use our recipe)

Sauté the shrimp with the onions in butter until warmed. Add thawed broccoli and water; heat to boiling; cover. Simmer, stirring once, 15 minutes or just until the broccoli is tender. Blend in the white sauce and add to the shrimp and broccoli mixture. Keep warmed while preparing our pancake recipe. For each serving put three pancakes together, with sauce between each.

TEXAS HASH

---

1 medium onion, chopped

1/2 cup green pepper, chopped

1/2 lb ground beef

1 8-oz can tomato sauce

1 8-oz can water

1/2 cup rice, uncooked, or 1 cup noodles, uncooked

1/2 t chili powder

dash pepper

dash salt

Sauté the onion and green pepper in oil. Add the ground beef and brown until all the red color is gone. Stir in the remaining ingredients. Pour into a casserole, cover and bake at 350° for 1 hour, removing the cover about 15 minutes before it is finished.

MOM'S (SCRATCH) SPAGHETTI SAUCE

Sauce

1 medium-size onion, chopped
6 cloves garlic, minced
3 6-oz cans tomato paste
3 cans water
1 29-oz can stewed tomatoes
3/4 cup vegetable oil (do not use olive oil)
2 bay leaves
fresh diced mushrooms
pepper to taste
oregano to taste

Meatballs*

1 lb ground round
1 egg
1/2 cup bread crumbs or 1/2 cup cooked rice
pepper to taste

Mix meatball ingredients together lightly with your hands. Form into meatballs. Sauté the onion and garlic in a very small amount of oil. Brown the meatballs in this mixture. Transfer these ingredients to a very large stock pot or deep kettle, add the rest of the ingredients, and mix gently. Simmer for 5 hours. This is an authentic Italian spaghetti recipe.

---

*You have the option of making meatballs or just adding ground beef to the sauce and having a meat sauce. If you prefer meatballs, we like to use ground round. To prepare the meatballs, follow the above instructions.

SWISS STEAK

1-1/4 lbs round steak, cut 3/4" thick

1-1/2 t salad oil

2 cloves garlic, crushed

Flour Mixture

1/4 cup flour

1 t salt

1/4 t pepper

Vegetables

1 raw onion, cut in 1/2 slices, 1/4" thick

1 bell pepper (cut in half and remove seeds and slice 1/4" lengthwise pieces)

2 stalks celery, sliced in 1/4" diagonal pieces

Tomato Mixture

1 1-lb can peeled whole tomatoes

1 6-oz can tomato paste

2 T brown sugar

scant salt

1/4 t black pepper

Combine the ingredients for the flour mixture. Set aside. Combine the ingredients for the tomato mixture. Set aside. Make vertical slits, 3" apart, in the fat side of the steak. Cut the meat into 4 or 5 serving pieces. Lay the pieces on a cutting board. Sprinkle half of the flour mixture on the meat. Pound each piece well with a mallet. Then turn the meat and sprinkle the rest of the flour, and pound to break up the tough connecting tissues, so that the meat is nice and tender. Heat the oil and garlic in a skillet, and remove the garlic. Fry both sides of the meat until well browned, and then remove the meat to a baking pan or casserole dish. Top the meat with the sliced vegetables and tomato mixture. Cover and bake at 350° for 1-1/2 hours, or until the meat is tender. Makes 4 servings.

TAMALE PIE

1 lb ground beef
1 cup chopped onion
1 cup chopped green pepper
2 8-oz cans tomato sauce
1 clove minced garlic
3 t chili powder
1 T sugar
dash pepper
1 cup corn
1 cup cooked carrots
1/2 cup sour cream (a maybe)
1 small (3 oz) pkg cream cheese (a maybe)
1/4 cup bread crumbs

Mix together the ground beef, onion and green pepper. Add the tomato sauce, garlic, chili powder, sugar and pepper. Simmer this for approximately 25 minutes. Then add the corn and carrots. Stir well, and add the sour cream and cream cheese. Place this in a buttered casserole dish and sprinkle the bread crumbs on top. Place in a 350° oven and bake for 40 minutes.

BARBECUED SPARERIBS OR CHICKEN WINGS

3 lb spareribs or chicken wings (chicken wings are better because you should not have pork)
1/2 cup ketchup
3/4 cup brown sugar
scant salt
1 clove garlic
1 small piece of ginger

Place chicken wings in pan. Combine all the remaining ingredients and pour over the chicken. Bake at 350° for 45 to 60 minutes. (If using ribs, cook at 275° for 2 hours.) Remove from pan and broil just before serving. Great as hors d'oeuvres.

HONEY-GLAZED GAME HENS

2 or 3 1-lb to 1-1/2-lb game hens
1/4 cup honey
2 T butter
1 T lemon juice
dash paprika (optional)
1 T sesame seeds (optional)

Prepare 2 or 3 games hens for roasting. Heat the butter in a small saucepan until it melts. Add the honey, lemon juice and paprika (if using). Bake the hens for 1/2 hour at 350°, uncovered. Brush with half the honey mixture, and return to oven for 15 minutes. Brush with remaining honey. Sprinkle the sesame seeds (optional) over the hens, and return to oven for 15 more minutes.

TEXAS POT ROAST
A MEAL IN ONE

3 lbs beef brisket, boneless round or chuck roast
1/3 cup flour
1/8 t pepper
1 cup chopped green onions
1-1/2 cups catsup
1/4 cup honey
2 T mustard
3 T brown sugar
3 T cider vinegar
1/2 cup water
4 carrots, sliced
4 potatoes, quartered
4 medium onions, chopped
8 mushrooms

Flour, season and puncture the beef of your choice. In a heavy skillet, brown the beef on both sides in 1 T corn or vegetable oil. Add the onions and cook until golden brown.

In a separate bowl, combine the catsup, honey, mustard, brown sugar, vinegar and water. Pour over the meat and bake, covered, for 2 hours at 275°. Then add the vegetables, spooning the sauce over them. Cook for one more hour. This has been a great favorite in our home!

AMBROSIA
(CHILLED FRUIT SALAD)

1 cup fresh sliced strawberries
1 cup fresh sliced peaches
1 cup fresh green grapes, cut in half
1 honeydew melon, scooped into little balls
1/4 of a watermelon, scooped into little balls
1 cantaloupe, scooped into little balls
1 cup mandarin oranges
1 cup fresh cherries, cut in half (if in season)
2 cups orange juice
1 fresh lemon, squeezed, and the juice reserved

Prepare all the fruit and chill together in a large salad bowl. Add the orange juice and the lemon juice to the mixture. Keep chilled until ready to serve.

AVOCADO AND CRAB SALAD ON A BED OF LETTUCE

1 lb crab legs, cooked, chilled and shelled

2 hard-cooked eggs, chopped

1/4 cup chopped celery

1/4 cup mayonnaise

1 t dry mustard

4 medium avocados

1 cup white grapes, sliced in two

Break crab meat into pieces; set aside several larger segments of meat for garnish. Combine remaining crab meat with eggs, celery, mayonnaise, mustard and grapes. Chill. When preparing the avocados, wait until just before you are ready to serve them to peel and stuff them. After you have peeled them, cut them in half. Tap your knife lightly on the seed and gently lift it out, leaving the meat intact. Rub the avocados with fresh lemon or lemon juice to keep them from discoloring. Stuff the avocados, and garnish with the reserved pieces of crab meat. Serve on lettuce leaves.

AVOCADO AND GRAPEFRUIT SALAD ON A BED OF LETTUCE

a chunk of cold, cooked shellfish (shrimp, lobster or crab)

grapefruit sections

one avocado, cleaned and halved

Combine the shellfish and grapefruit in portions to suit your taste. Place in the cavity of the avocado. Serve this on a bed of lettuce and top with cocktail sauce (recipe follows).

COCKTAIL SAUCE

1 cup yogurt

1/2 cup ketchup

1 T vegetable oil

1 T vinegar

1-1/2 t sugar

2 t paprika

Mix all ingredients together and chill. This makes about 1-1/2 cups.

YUMMY BEAN AND BROCCOLI SALAD

1 can green beans, drained
1 can kidney beans, drained and rinsed in cold water
1 can chick peas (garbanzo)
1/2 cup chopped celery
1 medium onion, chopped
1 green pepper, chopped
2 cups broccoli buds, rinsed
1 red pimiento (from a small jar)
1/2 cup vinegar
3/4 cup sugar
Dash pepper
1/2 cup salad oil
1 t salt

In a large bowl, combine the green beans, kidney beans, chick peas, celery, onion, green pepper, broccoli and pimiento. Mix well. Add the vinegar, sugar, pepper, salad oil and salt. Toss to coat well. This is a good summer quicky salad.

BERRY SALAD

2 small (3-oz) pkg strawberry jello

2 small boxes or one large bag frozen strawberries (or 2 cups fresh)

2 cups applesauce

3 cups hot water

2 t lemon juice

64 small marshmallows

1 box Dream Whip, prepared according to package directions

Dissolve the jello in hot water and add strawberries, applesauce, and lemon juice. Place in a 9 x 13 x 2-inch cake pan and let set overnight. Mix marshmallows with the Dream Whip and let set overnight. Frost salad with marshmallow mixture before serving.

CARROT SALAD

2 carrots
2 apples
1/2 cup raisins
1/2 cup yogurt, plain
1/4 cup Grape Nut cereal
1/4 t vegetable oil
1/2 t lemon juice
1/2 t sugar
touch of mustard

Grate carrots and apples together in a bowl. Add raisins, yogurt, oil, sugar, and mustard. Add the Grape Nuts and lemon juice shortly before serving. Serves 4.

COLESLAW

2 cups white vinegar
2 cups sugar
2 T mustard seed
1/2 t celery seed
1 large head of cabbage
6 small onions
2 green peppers
2 carrots

Heat vinegar, sugar, mustard seed and celery seed until sugar melts. Cool. Chop cabbage, onions, peppers and carrots. Mix all the ingredients together and chill. This is ready to serve as soon as it is cold. It may be stored in the refrigerator for up to a week.

CHICKEN SALAD

5 cups cubed chicken
2 cups sliced celery
1 medium onion
1 green bell pepper, slivered
2 medium kohlrabi or water chestnuts
sprinkles of herbs and parsley (preferably fresh)
homemade mayonnaise (recipe in this cookbook)

Cook a 3- or 4-pound chicken, adding the sprinkles of fresh or dried herbs and parsley to the cooking water. Cool chicken and debone it. Put the bones back in the broth and simmer a few minutes. Strain out the bones and save the broth. This broth is considered bouillon. Good for soup, etc. When the chicken has become solid, cube it, putting all scraps back into the broth. Now add the other ingredients and make the chicken salad. Add the mayonnaise dressing just before serving. Great served over lettuce with toast points and fruit.

FESTIVE FRUIT SALAD

2 3-oz pkg orange jello
2 16-oz cans apricots (reserve juice)
2 cups hot water
1 11-oz can mandarin oranges (reserve juice)
2 cups combined juice of apricots and oranges

Add boiling water to jello; stir to dissolve thoroughly. Add combined fruit juices. Chop apricots. (Should yield 1-1/2 cups.) Add fruit, and pour into oblong cake pan or your favorite mold. Let set.

SALAD TOPPING

1 cup juice (orange or apricot)
1 T butter
2-3 heaping T flour
1 egg
1/2 cup sugar
1 pkg Dream Whip

Mix juice, butter, flour, egg and sugar together and refrigerate until thick. Fold in 1 cup prepared Dream Whip and spread over the jello mixture. Drizzle a small amount of orange juice atop.

COMBINATION SALAD

---

head of lettuce, washed and shredded

2 oranges, separated into sections

2 bananas, sliced

2 apples, sliced

one bunch green grapes, each grape sliced in half

mayonnaise

Mix the oranges, bananas, apples and grapes, adding just enough mayonnaise to coat them lightly. Serve on the shredded lettuce.

LAYERED LETTUCE SALAD

1 head of lettuce, torn into bite-size pieces
1/2 cup diced green pepper
1/2 cup diced celery
1/2 cup green onions and tops
1 pkg frozen peas, separated
6 slices fried and crumbled Lean Strips or bacon substitute*
1/2 pkg fresh bean sprouts

Layer the above ingredients in a large bowl. Cover with the homemade mayonnaise (recipe found in this cookbook) and 3 T of sugar on top. Garnish with chives.

This particular salad is very good if made the night before.

---

*3 oz tiny bay shrimp may be substituted for the Lean Strips.

MARINATED SALAD

2 nectarines, sliced
1/2 lb mushrooms, quartered
1 cup cherry tomatoes, halved
1/3 cup green onion, cut in 1" lengths
1 jar artichoke hearts, drained
1/3 cup vegetable oil
1/4 cup lemon juice
1 t salt

Mix the above ingredients together and let set approximately 2 to 4 hours.

ORANGE JELLO SALAD

1 large pkg orange jello
1 cup hot water
2 cups apricot nectar
1 11-oz can mandarin oranges, drained
1 cup Dream Whip prepared as directed on package (we need this brand because it does not have any coconut in it)
1 cup small marshmallows

Mix the jello, water and apricot nectar until the liquid is as thick as syrup. Add the oranges, Dream Whip and marshmallows. Pour into an oiled 6-cup mold. Chill until set.

JUNE PEA SALAD

---

2 16-oz cans early June peas, drained (fresh are even
  better)

---

2 large ribs celery

3/4 cup substitute low-salt cheese (white)

---

5 green onions

1/4 t cracked black pepper

---

2 drops garlic juice

1/2 t prepared mustard

3/4 cup mayonnaise

Finely chop celery and onions. Cube the substitute cheese. Mix all the ingredients together. May be served immediately, but is much better if marinated
overnight.

HOT CREAMY
GERMAN POTATO SALAD

3-1/2 lbs potatoes (12 medium)
1 medium onion, chopped (1/2 cup)
2 T butter
1/4 cup sugar
2 T all-purpose flour
1 t pepper
1 cup water
1/3 cup vinegar
1 cup yogurt
sprig of parsley
1 T dill

Cook potatoes in boiling water for 35 minutes or until tender. Drain. Cook onions in butter until tender. Stir in sugar, flour and pepper. Add water and vinegar. Cook and stir until mixture is thick and bubbly. Remove from heat; stir in yogurt. Peel and slice warm potatoes; toss with the warm dressing and, if you can tolerate bacon, you may use a few crumbs to taste. (Remember bacon is a definite no-no, yet there are a few people who can tolerate it. This we will leave up to you.) Serve *hot* and garnish with a little dill and a sprig of parsley.

DOROTHY'S SHRIMP MACARONI SALAD

1/2 7-oz pkg (1 cup) macaroni (shells are great)

1 cup chopped celery

1/4 cup onion, chopped

1/4 cup green pepper, chopped

1/4 cup pimiento (optional), chopped

1 cup shrimp, preferably fresh-cooked (water-packed if canned)

2 hard-boiled eggs, chopped

1/4 t salt (optional)

1/4 t paprika

1 cup mayonnaise (recipe in this cookbook)

1/4 cup french dressing (recipe in this cookbook)

Cook macaroni. Drain and chill. Add celery, onion, green pepper, pimiento, shrimp and eggs. Add your seasonings and mix. Add the mayonnaise and french dressing and serve atop lettuce. Garnish with tomato slices. You may also use ingredients other than shrimp, like chicken, crab and even tuna. Serve on a bed of lettuce with a roll.

SPINACH SALAD

Salad

---

6 slices of crumbled substitute bacon (Lean Strips is a
good substitute)

---

2 hard-boiled eggs, chopped

---

1 pound fresh spinach

Dressing

1/2 cup sugar

1/2 cup light vinegar

---

2 T oil (salad)

---

1 T chopped green onion

---

1 T chopped parsley

---

1 T chopped chives

---

1 T prepared mustard

---

cracked black pepper to taste

---

1 cube of ice

Mix the salad dressing ingredients in a plastic container. Add an ice cube.
Shake well and chill. Pour over spinach, bacon substitute, and eggs. Season
to taste with pepper and salt at your discretion. Toss well and serve.

NOTE: This dressing keeps well for several days if kept in the refrigerator.
Serves six.

WILTED LEAF SALAD

---

6 bacon substitute slices (i.e., Lean Strips)

1 large head of leaf lettuce

1 medium onion, thinly sliced

1/4 cup light cider vinegar

1-1/2 t sugar

1/2 t dry mustard

1/4 t salt, depending on your limit

dash pepper

1 raw egg

2 hard-boiled eggs, sliced, for garnish

In a large skillet, fry the bacon substitute until crisp. Drain on paper towels. Discard all but 1/4 cup of bacon drippings. Tear lettuce into bite-size pieces. Crumble the bacon substitute and add to onion slices, tossing well. Into bacon drippings in skillet, stir the vinegar, sugar, mustard, salt, pepper and raw egg. Heat, stirring constantly, for a couple of seconds. Remove from heat to keep the egg from frying. Pour over lettuce mixture. Lettuce will become wilted. This is all right. Garnish with sliced hard-boiled eggs.

ZUCCHINI SALAD

4 medium zucchini, sliced
2 green onions, chopped fine
1 green pepper, chopped
1 stalk celery, chopped
1/3 cup sugar
3 T white vinegar
3 T vegetable oil
1/2 t fresh ground pepper

Mix the sugar, vinegar, oil, and pepper together and then add to the vegetables. Chill until you are ready to serve.

FRENCH DRESSING

1/2 cup olive oil
1/2 cup vegetable oil
1/4 cup cider vinegar
1/4 cup lemon juice
1/2 t salt
1/2 t dry mustard
1/2 t paprika
1/4 cup ketchup

Shake all ingredients together in an airtight jar. Keep covered in refrigerator; will keep for up to a week. Shake before using.

QUICK FRUIT DRESSING

1 cup sugar
juice and rind of 1 lemon and orange
1/8 t cream of tartar
1 egg, well beaten

Combine all ingredients in saucepan. Cook over medium heat, stirring constantly until boiling. Boil 1 minute. Remove from heat. Cool. Yields 1-1/2 cups of dressing. Very good atop fruit!

GREEK GODDESS DRESSING

3 T vinegar
1 T lemon juice
1 clove garlic, crushed and grated
ground pepper to taste
1 T celery seed
1/2 cup salad oil
2 T water

Shake all ingredients together in an airtight jar. Keep covered in refrigerator; will keep in refrigerator for up to a week. Shake well before using.

ITALIAN DRESSING

1/2 cup french dressing (recipe in this cookbook)
2 T sugar
1/2 t celery salt
1/2 t grated onion
1/4 t garlic juice
1/4 t ground pepper

Add the sugar, celery salt, onion, garlic juice and ground pepper to 1/2 cup of french dressing (recipe in this book). Shake all ingredients together in an airtight jar. Keep covered in refrigerator; will keep for up to one week. Shake before using.

CREAMY ITALIAN DRESSING

1/2 cup plain yogurt
1/4 t dry mustard
1 t confectioner's sugar
1/4 t fresh ground pepper
2 T vinegar
1/4 t liquid garlic

Shake all ingredients together in an airtight jar. Keep covered in refrigerator; will keep for up to one week. Shake before using.

MAYONNAISE

1 egg yolk
1 t dry mustard
1 t confectioner's sugar
1/4 t salt
cayenne pepper, dash
2 T cider vinegar
1 cup vegetable oil
1 cup whipping cream, whipped (a maybe)

Beat together with rotary beater the egg yolk, mustard, sugar, salt, cayenne, and 1 T of the vinegar. Continue beating while adding oil, at first drop by drop, then gradually increasing amount as mixture thickens until all is used. Slowly add the other T of vinegar. Beat well. Add already whipped whipping cream to the mixture at this time. Chill. Mix with salad just before serving. Very good with vegetables, meat and fruit salads. This is a good base for a lot of dressings. Yields 2-1/2 cups.

BASIC WHITE SAUCE

1 T margarine
1 T flour
1 cup chicken broth (if using canned, buy low salt broth—Campbell's has one)

Melt margarine in a saucepan over moderate heat. Add flour; stir and blend till smooth (may turn slightly brown). Slowly add broth. Cook till thickened.

PINK SAUCE

1 cup mayonnaise
1 cup chili sauce
1 t horseradish
4 minced sweet pickles
2 minced stalks of celery
1 minced small onion
4 minced green onions
4 minced sprigs parsley
1 T sugar

Blend all ingredients together. Refrigerate. Yields about 2-1/2 cups. It is really good as a shrimp dip or with any other seafood.

SOUR CREAM SALAD DRESSING

1 cup commercial sour cream (This is a maybe. You may substitute plain yogurt.)
3 T minced chives and onion
2 T lemon juice or 1 T vinegar
salt (depending on what you can handle)
1/8 t pepper

Combine all ingredients. Very good over raw onions and cucumbers. Also very good on baked potatoes.

THOUSAND ISLAND DRESSING

1/2 cup mayonnaise (recipe in this cookbook)
1 T chili sauce
3 large chopped stuffed olives (a maybe)
1 hard-boiled egg, minced
1/2 t paprika
pepper to taste
1 t sugar

Combine all ingredients; mix well. Good on greens and hot vegetables.

COLD CUCUMBER SOUP

---

4 cups cucumbers, peeled, seeded and diced

5 cups chicken stock (preferably ours)

5 T butter (unsalted)

4 T flour

3 cups light cream (remember this is a maybe)

salt and pepper to taste (salt is a maybe)

Peel, seed and dice the cucumbers. Set aside 1/2 cup of cucumber for garnish. Place the remaining 3-1/2 cups in a saucepan with 3 cups of the stock. Cook over moderate heat until the vegetable is tender. Melt the butter in a soup kettle, blend in the flour, and stir in the cream. Simmer over low heat for 3 minutes, stirring constantly. Stir in the remaining 2 cups of chicken stock and simmer for 3 more minutes. Adjust the seasonings and serve chilled. Garnish with the reserved cucumber and bread sticks. Serves 6 nice-size bowls of soup.

BASIC CREAM SOUPS

4 cups fresh vegetables, coarsely chopped
5 cups chicken stock
5 T butter
4 T flour
3-1/2 cups light cream (this is a maybe)
salt and pepper to taste (maybe on salt)
2 bay leaves (these are to be removed before the soup is served)

(Any allowable vegetable may be added to this to make it cream of asparagus, broccoli, artichoke, cucumber, spinach or cauliflower, whatever you decide you would like to have. That vegetable in that particular quantity may be added to this basic recipe and you will have that particular soup. It is a very easy recipe.)

Peel vegetables and chop to your desired size. Then place the vegetables with the stock in the saucepan and cook over medium heat until the vegetables are tender. Remove some of the vegetables and set them aside to use as garnish later. Puree the remaining cooked vegetables together with the vegetable water, in a blender or through a strainer. Melt the butter in a soup kettle and blend in the flour, making sort of a roux, and then stir in the cream. Simmer over low heat, stirring constantly for 3 minutes. Adjust the seasonings to your own individual taste and garnish each bowl with the reserved cooked vegetables. You may serve any of these hot or cold.

Any of the following vegetables may be used: artichokes, asparagus, avocados, broccoli, Brussels sprouts, celery, cucumbers, leeks, mushrooms, onions, potatoes or spinach.

MOM'S VEGETABLE BEEF SOUP

1-1/2 lb stew beef or chuck or soup bone
1 t salt (beware of what your salt load is)
1/2 t pepper
2 bay leaves
1/2 t oregano
1/2 cup chopped onion
1 cup chopped celery
1 cup chopped cabbage
4 or 5 medium sliced carrots
5 medium fresh tomatoes, skinned and sliced

Cover meat with cold water in a heavy 3-qt kettle. Add salt, pepper, bay leaves and oregano. Let it come to a boil while preparing the vegetables. Turn heat low and add onion, celery, carrots and cabbage. Simmer at least 2-1/2 hours or until meat is very tender. Remove bone and bay leaves and cut meat into bite-size pieces. Add the tomatoes, let simmer for an hour longer and serve. Actually, the longer you cook this, the better it tastes.

OLD-FASHIONED ONION SOUP

5 T butter

3-1/2 cups sliced onions

9 cups beef consomme (recipe follows)

1 cup flour

freshly ground pepper to taste

1 cup grated substitute cheese

1 egg

Consomme (beef stock or bouillon)

3 lb beef or veal bones

2 lb beef meat (lean)

4 medium onions, chopped

3 carrots, chopped

2 celery stalks, diced

4 qts of water

2 t salt

6 peppercorns

4 t dried or fresh parsley

Combine the lean meat, beef and veal bones in a large pot. Add the 4 qts of water and bring to a boil. Remove the scum that rises to the surface. Clean and prepare the vegetables. Add the vegetables and the spices to the kettle, and simmer for about 4 hours. At this time you may alter the seasonings to your own taste. Strain the bouillon through a colander and then through a cheese cloth. (I save the vegetables and meat for a stew and throw away the bones.) Pour the bouillon into covered containers, cool and refrigerate. After it has cooled, you may notice sediment again at the top. This should be removed before using the consomme in your onion soup recipe, or any other for that matter. This is a good basic consomme recipe.

You can keep this refrigerated for up to a week or you may keep this in the freezer for 2 to 3 weeks. This yields 10 servings.

To make the onion soup, melt the butter and sauté the sliced onion until limp and transparent. Pour the consomme into a large pot and bring to a boil. Add the sautéed onions and simmer for 15 minutes. While the soup is simmering, measure the flour in a bowl and mix in the egg. Cut the dough into small pieces. Dry these pieces on a bread board for about 10 minutes. Rub the pieces of dough between your palms until they crumble into the simmering soup pot. Simmer 10 more minutes. Taste again for seasoning. Pour into individual soup crocks. Sprinkle with the grated cheese substitute and place in a 300° oven to keep warmed until you are ready to serve.

BAKED ONION SOUP

Onion soup

1 T oil
4 T butter
3 lb sweet onions, peeled and sliced thin
salt and ground pepper to taste
3 T flour
2 qt homemade beef or chicken stock, heated
1 bay leaf
1/2 t dried thyme
1 t fresh chopped parsley

Croutons

This portion of the recipe may only be used if you do not have a reaction to cheese or if you have found a cheese substitute. Kraft suggested to us that they may have one out in 1983.
2 slices of french bread per serving
cheese substitute
1 egg yolk
2 T light cream
dash of salt
pepper to taste

Slice the onions thin and sauté them in a large pot with the melted oil and butter. Cook over low heat, stirring occasinally until the onions become transparent. This will take approximately 30 minutes. Add the salt and pepper if desired. When onions have reached transparency, stir in the flour and cook over low heat for 2 more minutes. Add the stock, bay leaf, dried thyme and parsley. Simmer the above while preparing your croutons. Mix the cheese substitute into a pastelike substance with the egg yolk, cream, salt and pepper. Put the slices of french bread in a 350° oven until they are brown. Spread the cheese mixture over half the slices. Set the other half aside. Put the onion soup in individual serving dishes. You will do this whether you use the above croutons or not. Place a slice of the substitute cheese-topped bread on top of soup. Place back in the oven and bake for about 10 minutes at 350°. Butter the remaining half of bread; put under broiler of the oven and brown. Cut up this toasted bread in cubes and garnish the soup with them. Serve these in a side dish, too. You especially should use these croutons if you cannot use the cheese-coated ones.

BARLEY-YOGURT SOUP

1 cup barley
6 cups chicken broth, preferably homemade
1 cup onion, chopped
1/4 cup butter
2 T dried mint
2 T fresh parsley, minced
pepper (freshly ground, to taste)
1 qt plain yogurt

Place the barley and the broth in a soup kettle and cook for 30 minutes. Peel and chop the onion; sauté in butter until transparent. Add this to the broth, along with the mint, parsley and pepper. Cook the soup over low heat until the barley is tender. Stir in the yogurt and continue to simmer for about 10 minutes. This soup can be served either icy cold or hot.

APPLE POUND CAKE

(This is a Blue Ribbon recipe.)

3 cups unsifted flour
1 t baking soda
1/2 t ground cinnamon
1/2 t nutmeg
1-1/2 cups corn oil
2 cups sugar
3 eggs
2 t imitation vanilla
2 cups finely chopped pared apples
2 cups chopped macadamia nuts
1/2 cup raisins
1/2 cup applejack or apple cider
1/4 cup brown sugar
2 T butter

Combine the flour with the baking soda, cinnamon and nutmeg; set aside. Beat together the oil, sugar, eggs and vanilla until thoroughly combined. Gradually beat the flour mixture into this until smooth. Fold in the apples, nuts and raisins. Turn into a greased and floured 10" tube pan. Bake at 325° for an hour and 15 minutes, or until the cake tester comes out clean.

As soon as the cake comes out of the oven, combine the applejack (or apple cider), brown sugar, and butter in a saucepan. Bring to a boil, and continue to boil until the sugar is completely dissolved. Then poke holes in the top of the still-warm cake, and spoon the hot syrup over it. Cool the cake on a rack for about 10 minutes. When it is cool, remove it from the pan and store it in an airtight container.

SPRING GLOW ANGEL CAKE

1 box angel food cake mix
1 4-oz pkg vanilla pudding
2 cups milk (okay because it will be cooked)
1 22-oz can peach pie filling
1 cup heavy cream, whipped

Prepare and bake cake mix according to package directions. Use a 10" tube pan. Cool and remove from pan. Slice entire top from cake about 1" down. Hollow center out, leaving an inch base and sides. Prepare pudding as directed, using 2 cups milk. When pudding has cooled, add half of pie filling and blend well. Spoon mixture into the cavity of the cake. Replace the top. Fold remaining pie filling into whipped cream and frost the cake. Chill and serve.

CAROB BROWNIES

(You may wish to double this recipe.)

3/4 cup flour

1/4 t baking soda

1/3 cup butter

3/4 cup sugar

2 T water

6 oz or 1 cup carob chips

1 t imitation vanilla

2 eggs

Combine the flour and baking soda and set aside. Bring the butter, sugar and water to a boil in a sauce pan. Remove from heat and add carob and vanilla. Stir until smooth and transfer the carob mix into a bowl. Add eggs one at a time. Then blend in the flour mixture. Bake in a 325° oven in a 9 by 9 greased pan for 35 minutes. Cool completely before you cut into this or your brownies will be gummy.

GRANDMA'S FAVORITE
APPLE BUNDT CAKE

3 cups unsifted flour
1 t salt
1/2 t ground cinnamon
1/2 t nutmeg
1-1/2 cups corn oil
2 cups sugar
3 eggs
2 t vanilla
2 cups finely chopped pared apples
2 cups raisins
1/2 cup apple juice
1/4 cup brown sugar
2 T butter or margarine

Sift together the flour, salt, cinnamon and nutmeg. Beat together oil, sugar, eggs and vanilla at medium speed of an electric mixer until thoroughly combined. Gradually beat in flour mixture until smooth. Fold in apples and raisins. Turn into greased and floured 10" bundt pan. Bake at 375° for one hour and 15 minutes, or until cake tester comes out clean.

As soon as the cake comes out of the oven, combine the apple juice, brown sugar and butter or margarine in a saucepan. Bring to a boil. Stir until sugar is dissolved. Prick top of cake and spoon syrup over the cake. Cool cake on wire rack for 10 minutes. Remove from pan. Store in airtight container when cool.

APPLESAUCE CAKE

1 pkg yellow cake mix
1 small pkg (4-1/8 oz) vanilla instant pudding mix
1/2 cup raisins
1 t cinnamon
1-1/2 cups applesauce
1/4 cup vegetable oil
3 eggs, well beaten

Mix all the above ingredients with a fork for 1 minute. Pour into an ungreased cake pan, 9 x 13 x 2. Bake at 350° for 35 to 40 minutes. If in a glass loaf pan, bake for 35 minutes. Cool in pan. Cut into squares and serve.

APPLE TORTE

1/2 cup shortening
2 cups sugar
2 eggs, beaten
4 cups raw diced apples
1 t baking soda
1 t salt—depends on your salt limit
1 t cinnamon
1/2 cup flour
1/4 cup oatmeal

Combine the shortening, sugar, eggs and apples. Stir well, then add the baking soda, salt, cinnamon, flour and oatmeal. Place the batter in a 9 x 9 pan, and bake at 350° for 45 minutes.

BANANA LOAF CAKE

2-1/4 cups sifted cake flour
1 cup sugar
2 t baking powder
1 t salt
1/2 cup shortening
1 t imitation vanilla
5 egg yolks, unbeaten
1/2 cup milk
1/4 cup milk
1/2 cup raisins
2 mashed bananas

Sift together the first four ingredients. Add the following four ingredients and beat for two minutes. Add the additional 1/4 cup milk and beat two more minutes. Fold the mashed bananas and the raisins into the mixture. Bake at 350° for 60-70 minutes in a 9 x 5 x 3 pan.

CAROB ZUCCHINI CAKE

2-1/4 cups sifted cake flour

1 cup sugar

2 t baking powder

2 eggs

2-1/2 cups unsifted flour

4 T powdered carob

1 t baking soda

1/2 t cinnamon

1/2 t cloves

1/2 cup sour cream (sour your own cream—add 1 t vinegar to 1/2 cup cream)

1 T vanilla

2 cups grated zucchini

2 cups carob chips

Cream margarine, oil and sugar. Add eggs one at a time, beating well after each addition. Combine dry ingredients and add to margarine mixture alternately with sour cream. Mix well after each addition. Add vanilla and mix. Add zucchini and combine until just mixed. Pour into 9 × 13 × 2 oiled glass baking disk. Sprinkle top with carob chips. Bake at 325° for 40-45 minutes. Cool in pan. Cut into squares and serve.

CARROT PUDDING CAKE

1 pkg yellow cake mix
1 pkg vanilla-flavored instant pudding and pie filling mix
4 eggs
1/3 cup water
1/4 cup oil
3 cups grated carrots
1/2 cup raisins, finely chopped
1/2 t salt
2 t ground cinnamon

Blend all ingredients in bowl. Beat 4 minutes at medium speed. Pour into two greased and floured 8 × 4 inch loaf pans. Bake at 350° for 45 to 50 minutes. Do not overbake. Cool in pan 15 minutes. Remove and cool on racks. Frost with orange cream cheese frosting.

ORANGE CREAM CHEESE FROSTING

1 3-oz pkg cream cheese (a maybe)
1/2 cup powdered sugar
2 T butter
1/8 cup orange juice

Combine the cream cheese, powdered sugar, butter and orange juice, and drizzle over the warm carrot pudding cake.

CHERRY TORTE

Crust

1 heaping cup flour
1 T sugar
1 stick butter or margarine

Mix the above together and pat in pie tin and brown at 350° (approximately 5-8 minutes).

Filling

1 8-oz pkg cream cheese
1 cup confectioner's sugar

Prepare 1 package of Dream Whip and fold into the above mixture. Pour into cool crust and top with prepared cherry pie filling. Chill.

COFFEE ROYAL CAKE

Batter

---

1 small box yellow cake mix

---

1 small box carob cake mix (Manna Mixins is a good
 brand to use)

Filling and Topping

1-1/2 cups heavy cream (a maybe)

---

3 T instant coffee

1/3 cup sugar

---

1 11-oz jar raspberry preserves

---

1 cup heavy cream (a maybe)

---

shaved carob chips (available at health food stores)

Prepare each cake mix according to package directions. Bake in 9" cake
pans. Cool and split each layer crosswire, forming two carob layers and
two yellow layers. Combine the heavy cream with the instant coffee and
sugar. Chill thoroughly, including bowl. Whip cream until stiff. Place one
yellow layer on serving plate. Spread with half of the raspberry preserves
and add a carob layer. Spread that with half of the coffee filling, then top it
with the other yellow cake layer. Spread the filling and preserves on that,
then end with the second carob layer. Finally, garnish with whipped cream
and shaved carob chips. Keep refrigerated until ready to serve.

FLAN

3/4 cup sugar

6 cups milk

4 eggs, separated

1 t imitation vanilla

dash nutmeg

Mix the sugar and milk; heat in a small saucepan (do not boil). Beat the egg yolks. Add a little of the milk mixture to the egg yolks. Add the egg mixture to the milk mixture, stirring constantly. Beat egg whites until stiff but not dry. Fold into yolk mixture. Add vanilla. Stir to mix. Pour into custard cups or a mold. Sprinkle with nutmeg. Set in a pan of hot water in a preheated 350° oven and cook until set. (Start checking after 20 minutes.) When flan is done, a knife inserted into the center should come out clean. Serve either warm or cold with caramel sauce. (Recipe follows.)

CARAMEL SAUCE

1 cup sugar
1 cup boiling water

Heat the sugar in a heavy iron skillet, stirring constantly until completely melted and light brown. Add water and bubble gently for 5 minutes, stirring occasionally. Remove from heat, and cool. Pour over individual servings of flan.

GINGERBREAD
"KIDS LOVE IT"

3/4 cup butter

1/2 cup sugar

1 egg

1/2 cup corn syrup (dark)

1/2 t baking soda

1-1/2 cups flour

1/2 t ginger

1 t cinnamon

1/2 cup sour milk (1/2 cup regular milk with 1 t vinegar
   in it)

Cream butter, sugar and egg. Beat syrup and soda until it foams and add to first mixture. Sift the flour and spices. Add alternately with the buttermilk substitute, which consists of the milk and vinegar. Line the bottom of a greased 8 × 8 inch pan with waxed paper. Grease paper. Bake at 350° for about 30 minutes or until tester comes out clean. Dust the warm gingerbread with powdered sugar, or top with Tangy Lemon Sauce. (Recipe follows.)

TANGY LEMON SAUCE

1 cup water
1/2 cup sugar
1/2 t lemon rind
2-1/2 T lemon juice
1 T butter
1 T cornstarch
small amount cold water

Dissolve sugar in water in a small saucepan, bring to a boil and boil for 5 minutes. Add lemon rind, lemon juice and butter; stir to mix. Dissolve cornstarch in cold water and slowly stir into hot mixture. Continue to boil and stir until slightly thickened. Cool till just warm and serve over gingerbread.

MACADAMIA NUT CAKE

1/2 lb butter

2 cups sugar

5 eggs

2 cups flour, sifted

1 t imitation vanilla

1 cup macadamia nuts (if nuts are salted, the salt should be washed off)

2 T flour

Cream butter and sugar well. Add one egg and a small part of flour, beating mixture constantly. Continue alternating flour and eggs until all ingredients are used and well mixed into batter. Add vanilla. Dredge nuts in 2 T flour and mix into the batter. Pour into a greased and floured tube pan. Bake one hour at 350°. Cool cake slightly before removing from the pan.

NOTE: Macadamia nuts are considered a questionable trigger to some people. You may wish to try a few at a time to consider your reaction and determine your limit.

MOCHA CAKE

Batter

6 large eggs
1 cup sugar
1 cup flour
2 T fine sifted instant coffee
2 T carob powder
1/2 cup unsalted butter (melted)
1 t imitation vanilla

Beat eggs and sugar on high for 12 minutes. They will triple in bulk and look like whipped cream. Sift and add flour, coffee and carob, 1/4 cup at a time, over egg mixture. Gently fold each addition by hand. Add the cooled, melted butter and vanilla, again folding in very carefully. Pour batter into 3 8" greased and floured pans. Bake at 350° for 15 to 20 minutes or until cake tests done. Turn out of pan at once and cool. Brush cake with warm Simple Syrup, then frost with Mocha Cream Frosting. (Recipes follow.)

SIMPLE SYRUP

1 cup sugar
1/2 cup water

Combine the above ingredients and bring just to a boil. Set aside until slightly cooled.

MOCHA CREAM FROSTING

---

3 sticks butter, softened

1-1/2 cups powdered sugar

2 egg yolks, slightly beaten

2 t vanilla

1 T instant powdered coffee

1 t water

1 5-oz can macadamia nuts, washed and chopped (optional)

Blend the above ingredients. The macadamia nuts are optional as they are a possible trigger. Including them depends on your reaction to them. When the cake has cooled, spread the frosting between the layers and on top.

POUND CAKE

1 cup butter
2 cups sugar
4 eggs
1 t vanilla flavoring (not extract)
1 t almond flavoring
1 t lemon flavoring
3 cups cake flour
1/2 cup milk

Cream butter and sugar until fluffy. Add eggs one at a time, beating after each addition. Add vanilla, almond and lemon flavoring. Fold in flour and milk alternately. Bake in a greased bundt pan at 325° for about one hour or until cake tests done. Cool for 10 minutes in pan, then turn out onto serving plate.

NOTE: It is important to use flavoring in place of extract because of the content of alcohol in the extract.

SOCK IT TO ME CAKE

---

1 20-oz pkg white cake mix

1 cup sour cream

3/4 cup Wesson oil

1/2 cup granulated sugar

4 eggs, beaten

3 T brown sugar

2 t cinnamon

1 cup raisins

1 cup powdered sugar

2 t butter

2 T boiled milk

Combine the first four ingredients well. Add one egg at a time, mixing well after each addition. Grease and flour a bundt pan. Pour half of the cake batter into the pan. Mix the brown sugar, cinnamon and raisins in a separate bowl. Sprinkle evenly over the first half of the batter. Top with remaining batter. Bake at 300° for one hour or until done. When the cake is done, remove from pan. Combine the powdered sugar, butter and milk. Mix until smooth. Frost the cake with this mixture.

FRESH STRAWBERRY CAKE (STRAWBERRY SWEETHEART CAKE)

Batter

1 20-oz box white cake mix
1 3-oz box strawberry jello
3/4 cup Wesson oil
3/4 cup milk
4 eggs, separated
1 cup chopped macadamia nuts (unsalted)
2 cups fresh strawberries, halved, or 2 4-oz pkg frozen strawberries, thawed and drained

Combine cake mix and jello. Mix together by hand. Add oil, milk and egg yolks. Beat just enough to mix. In a separate bowl, mix nuts and strawberries. Put half of this mixture in batter, reserving the remaining half for frosting. Beat egg whites until stiff but not dry. Fold into batter. Pour into three 8- or 9-inch greased and floured cake pans. Bake 20 to 25 minutes at 350°. Cool 10 minutes in pan, then turn onto rack and cool completely.

Frosting

1/2 stick of margarine, softened
1 16-oz box powdered sugar
1/2 strawberry mixture (see instructions above)

Cream margarine. Stir in powdered sugar. Add remaining half of strawberry mixture and beat well. Ice the cooled cake.

GOOD LUCK WHITE CAKE

1 20-oz Duncan Hines white cake mix
1/2 cup sugar
3/4 cup buttery Wesson oil
4 eggs
1 8-oz carton sour cream
1 t vanilla flavoring

Put cake mix into mixing bowl. Add remaining ingredients in order given and beat well. Grease and flour two 9″ pans. Divide batter in half and pour into pans. Bake at 350° for 20 to 25 minutes or until the cake tests done. Do not overbake. When done, cool for 5 minutes in the pan. Turn out and ice with Seven-Minute Icing. (Recipe in this book.)

APPLE SQUARES

Dough

1 cup butter or margarine
3/4 cup sugar
3 egg yolks
pinch salt
3 cups flour
1 t baking powder

Filling

1-3/4 cups apple slices, drained
3/4 t cinnamon
1/4 t cloves
1 cup sugar

Cream the butter and sugar. Add egg yolks and dry ingredients. Mix well; batter will be stiff. Divide the dough into two batches. Pat one batch of dough in a greased square pan. Mix the filling and pour it over the dough. Pat the other batch of dough over the filling and bake in a 350° oven until brown, about 1 hour. While still hot, cut into squares and sprinkle powdered sugar over the top.

OATMEAL-CAROB CHIP COOKIES

1/2 cup granulated sugar

1/4 cup packed brown sugar

1/4 cup unsalted butter

1/4 cup shortening

1 egg

1 t light vanilla

1 cup all-purpose flour

1/2 t salt

1/2 t baking soda

2 T milk

1 cup quick-cooking rolled oats

1 6-oz pkg carob pieces

In a mixing bowl, cream the sugars, butter, shortening, egg and vanilla. Stir together the flour, salt and baking soda, and then combine the creamed mixture with them. Add the milk, and stir in the oats and carob pieces. Prepare your cookie sheets by greasing them with shortening. Drop cookie dough from teaspoon 2 inches apart on cookie sheet. Bake in 375° oven for 8 minutes. Let stand a short time before removing from the cookie sheet. This recipe makes approximately 3 dozen.

CAROB CHIP COOKIES

1 cup unsalted butter
1 t baking soda
1 t salt
1 cup brown sugar
1 cup white sugar
3 eggs
2 cups flour
2 cups oatmeal
1 cup carob chips

Add all of the above ingredients in the sequence that you see them, and mix them together. Drop them by rounded teaspoonfuls onto an ungreased cookie sheet, and bake at 350° for approximately 10 minutes. Remove from pan and cool on linen paper or cooling racks before storing in cookie jar.

CARROT-RAISIN COOKIES

1 cup sugar
1/2 cup shortening
1 egg, unbeaten
1/2 cup raw carrots, grated
1/2 cup raisins
2 cups flour
2 t baking powder
1/2 t salt
1 t imitation vanilla

Mix all the ingredients. (Batter is very stiff; you may wish to use your hands to mix it.) Drop by teaspoonfuls on a greased baking sheet. Bake 10 to 12 minutes at 375°. Yields 36 cookies.

CARROT COOKIES

2 cups shredded carrots
3/4 cup unsalted softened butter
1 cup sugar
1 egg
1 t imitation vanilla
2 cups all-purpose flour
2 t baking powder
1/4 t salt

Cook carrots in a small amount of boiling water till tender. Drain and mash. This should be equivalent to one cup. Cool the carrots. Cream butter and sugar. Add the egg and vanilla; beat till fluffy. Stir in mashed carrots. Stir together flour, baking powder, and salt. Blend this into the batter. Drop batter from a teaspoon onto an ungreased cookie sheet. Bake at 375° for 10-12 minutes. Cool and spread with a powdered sugar frosting.

MINT-CAROB REFRIGERATOR COOKIES

1/2 cup unsalted butter, softened

1/2 cup granulated sugar

1 egg

1 t vanilla

1-3/4 cup all-purpose flour

1/2 t baking powder

1/2 t salt

1/2 cup carob powder (you may find this product in Safeway stores or other grocery/health food stores)

1/4 cup finely crushed peppermint candy

Cream together the butter, sugar, egg and vanilla. Stir together the dry ingredients and combine with the creamed mixture. Now add the carob powder and the mint candy. Shape the dough in two 6-inch rolls. Wrap in clear plastic wrap. Chill at least 4 hours or overnight. Cut in thin slices; place on ungreased cookie sheet. Bake in 375° oven for 8 minutes. This recipe makes approximately 4 dozen cookies.

MOM'S OLD-FASHIONED ICE BOX COOKIES

Batter

1/2 cup unsalted butter
1/2 cup sugar
1/4 cup light molasses
1 egg
1 t imitation vanilla
2 cups flour
1/2 t baking powder
1/2 t salt

Date Filling

1 cup finely chopped pitted dates
1/4 cup sugar
1/4 cup water
1/4 cup diced raisins
1 t lemon juice
1 t vanilla

Cream the butter, sugar, molasses, egg and vanilla. Gradually add the flour, baking powder and salt to the mixture, blending thoroughly. Chill 45 minutes while making date filling.

Combine the dates, sugar and water. Bring to a boil. Cook and stir over low heat till thick. Remove from heat and stir in the raisins, lemon juice and vanilla. Let this mixture cool slightly before spreading on the cookie dough.

On waxed paper, roll the chilled dough to 12 x 10 inch rectangle. Spread with date filling. Now roll the dough, beginning at the long end, and pinch the edges to seal. Cut the roll in half. Wrap in clear plastic and chill. When you are ready to use, cut the dough roll in thin slices and place on greased cookie sheet. Bake in a 375° oven for approximately 8 minutes. This recipe makes approximately 4 dozen cookies.

APRICOT-BRAN DELIGHTS

3/4 cup finely chopped dried apricots
1/2 cup orange juice
1/2 cup whole bran cereal
1/2 cup unsalted, softened butter
1/2 cup packed brown sugar
1 egg
1 t imitation vanilla
1-1/2 cups all-purpose flour
1 t ground cinnamon

Pour boiling water over apricots and allow to cool. Mix juice and cereal and let stand for a few minutes. Cream butter, sugar, egg and vanilla. Stir in cereal mixture with creamed mixture. Stir together dry ingredients with creamed mixture. Drain apricots well and fold into the creamed mixture. Drop from teaspoon on greased cookie sheet. Bake at 375° approximately 10 minutes, or until light brown.

FROSTED ORANGE DROPS

3/4 cup shortening
1/4 cup unsalted butter
1-1/2 cups packed brown sugar
2 eggs
1 cup plain yogurt
2 T grated orange peel
1/4 cup orange juice
1 t vanilla
3-1/2 cups all-purpose flour
2 t baking powder
1 t baking soda
1/4 t salt

Cream together the first 3 ingredients and beat in the eggs. Slowly beat in the yogurt, peel, juice, and vanilla. Stir together the dry ingredients, and blend into the batter. Drop from teaspoon on greased cookie sheet. Bake at 350° for about 15 minutes. Makes 8 dozen cookies.

ORANGE FROSTING

---

2 cups powdered sugar

2 T concentrated orange juice

1 t melted butter

Blend all ingredients until smooth; drizzle over warm orange drop cookies.

LACY OATMEAL CRISPS

---

1 cup packed brown sugar

1/2 cup shortening

1/4 cup butter

2-1/4 cup rolled oats

1/2 t baking soda

1/4 t salt

1 egg, beaten

In a saucepan, combine the brown sugar, shortening, and butter. Cook over low heat, stirring often, until melted. Remove from heat. Stir in the rolled oats, baking soda, and salt. Add the beaten egg, mixing well. Drop batter from a teaspoon onto an ungreased cookie sheet, 3 inches apart. Stir remaining batter often. Bake at 375° for 6-7 minutes. Cool on rack, then remove gently.

APPLE BUTTER-OATMEAL BARS

1/2 cup unsalted butter
1/2 cup brown sugar
1/2 cup apple butter (be sure to check the ingredients on the label)
1 egg
2/3 cup all-purpose flour
1/2 t baking soda
1/2 t baking powder
1/4 t salt
1 cup quick-cooking rolled oats

Cream the butter and sugar and blend in the apple butter and egg. Mix together the flour, baking soda, baking powder and salt, and blend with the creamed mixture. Stir in the oats. Spread in a greased 13 x 9 x 2 inch baking pan. Bake at 350° for 20 minutes. Sprinkle powdered sugar over top while warm. Cool and cut into bars.

BANANA-CAROB BARS

3/4 cup unsalted butter, softened

3/4 cup granulated sugar

2/3 cup packed brown sugar

1 egg

1 t vanilla

2 ripe medium bananas, mashed (equivalent to 1 cup)

2 cups all-purpose flour

2 t baking powder

1/2 t salt

1 6-oz pkg carob chips

Cream together the butter, sugar, and brown sugar. Add the egg and vanilla. Mix in the mashed banana. Combine the flour, baking powder and salt, and add to the creamed mixture. Stir in the carob chips. Spread in a greased and floured 15-1/2 x 10-1/2 x 1 inch baking pan. Bake at 350° for approximately 25 minutes. Cool and cut into bars.

FIG CHEWY BARS

1/2 cup unsalted butter
1 cup packed brown sugar
3 eggs
2 t grated lemon peel
1 t vanilla
1 cup all-purpose flour
1 t baking powder
1/2 t salt
2 cups finely diced dried figs

Cream butter and sugar. Add the eggs, lemon peel and vanilla; beat well. Stir together flour, baking powder and salt, then blend this into the creamed mixture. Stir in the diced figs. Pour batter into a shortening-greased 13 x 9 x 2 inch baking pan. Bake at 350° for 25 minutes. Cool and cut into bars.

LEMON BARS

---

1 cup all-purpose flour

1/4 cup sifted powdered sugar

1/2 cup unsalted butter

2 eggs

1 cup granulated sugar

1/2 t shredded lemon peel

3 T lemon juice

2 T all-purpose flour

1/4 t baking powder

powdered sugar

Stir together the flour and the powdered sugar. Add the softened butter to the mixture, and pat into an ungreased 8 x 8 x 2 inch baking pan. Bake at 350° for 10 to 12 minutes, being careful not to overbake.

In a mixing bowl, beat the eggs. Add the granulated sugar, lemon peel and juice. Beat till slightly thick and smooth. This may take 8-10 minutes. In a separate bowl, stir together the 2 T of flour and the baking powder. Add this to the egg mixture. Blend just till everything is moistened. Pour this over the baked layer. Bake at 350° for 20-25 minutes. Sift powdered sugar over top. Cool and cut into bars.

APRICOT BARS

3/4 cup unsalted butter, softened

1/2 cup sifted powdered sugar

1/4 t almond extract

1-3/4 cup all-purpose flour

1/2 t salt

1 12-oz jar apricot preserves

1/2 cup finely chopped candied fruit and peels

Cream the butter, powdered sugar, and almond extract. Stir together the flour and salt, and add to the creamed mixture. Mix till crumbly. Reserve 1 cup for topping, and pat the remainder into an ungreased 13 x 9 x 2 inch baking pan. Now combine the preserves and the candied fruit/peels. Spread this over the crumb layer. Top with the cup of reserved crumbs. Bake at 350° till golden, about 30 to 35 minutes. Cut the bars while still warm.

FESTIVE MINCEMEAT GOODIES

1 9-oz pkg instant condensed mincemeat
1 14-oz can sweetened condensed milk
1/2 cup unsalted, softened butter
1 cup packed brown sugar
1 T milk
1-3/4 cup finely crushed cornflakes
1 cup all-purpose flour
1 t baking soda

In a saucepan crumble mincemeat; add sweetened condensed milk. Cook, stirring till thickened (about 5 minutes); remove from heat.

Cream butter, brown sugar, and milk till fluffy. In a separate bowl, stir cornflakes with flour and baking soda. Add to creamed mixture and mix this well. Pat half of the crumb mixture into an ungreased 13 x 9 x 2 inch baking pan. Carefully spread the mincemeat mixture. Sprinkle the remaining crumb mixture over the top, and bake in a 350° oven for about 30 minutes. Cool and cut into bars.

DATE BARS

1 cup sugar
1 cup flour
1 t baking powder
1/2 t salt
1 t imitation vanilla flavoring
2 cups chopped dates or other chopped fruit
1/2 cup finely chopped macadamia nuts
3 eggs, separated

Sift the dry ingredients together and heat the yolks until thick and lemon-colored. Add vanilla. Add dry ingredients and mix thoroughly. Add fruit and nuts. Fold in stiffly beaten egg whites. Spread about 1/2" thick in greased baking pan and bake at 325° for about 25 minutes. When cool, cut in strips and roll in powdered sugar. This should yield approximately 30 bars.

ENGLISH TOFFEE

1 cup margarine or butter
1 cup sugar
1 egg yolk
1 t imitation vanilla
2 cups flour
1 egg white
1/2 cup macadamia nuts, chopped

Cream the margarine and sugar well. Add egg yolk and beat. Add vanilla and flour and mix. Spread in a jelly roll pan (10 by 15). Beat the egg white until fluffy and spread over the cookie dough. Sprinkle chopped nuts and press in lightly. Bake at 275° for 1 hour or until light brown. Cut while hot into 1 by 1-1/2" pieces.

TRADITIONAL ICEBOX COOKIES

1 cup shortening (lard, butter or margarine)
2 cups brown sugar, firmly packed
2 eggs, well beaten
1 t vanilla
3 to 3-1/2 cups sifted bread flour
1 t baking soda
scant salt

Cream the shortening. Add sugar gradually and cream this thoroughly. Add the beaten eggs and the imitation vanilla. Sift the dry ingredients and mix in. The dough should be stiff enough to handle; do not add too much flour. Use plain or divide it into two parts and vary by adding raisins or dates or some kind of a spice mixture. Even melted carob is good. Shape into rolls or press into loaves in a bread pan and chill overnight or at least 7 hours, until it is hard and cold. Bring out one at a time. Slice very thin with a sharp knife. Bake in a hot oven (350°) until slightly brown.

MACADAMIA NUT BUTTER CRISP

1 cup butter

1 cup sugar

1 egg, separated

2 cups flour

3/4 t ground mace

scant salt

1 cup macadamia nut bits (If you cannot buy these unsalted, then wash the salt off the nuts.)

Cream the butter and sugar and beat in the egg yolk thoroughly. Sift the flour with the mace and salt and add to the creamed mixture and beat thoroughly. Spread it in an even layer over entire surface of jelly roll pan (10 by 15"). Beat egg white slightly. Spread over the top. Sprinkle the nuts over the surface, pressing them into the dough. Bake in a slow oven (about 275°) for an hour or until they are lightly browned. Cut into 1-1/2" squares while hot. This makes approximately four dozen.

CAROB TOLLHOUSE COOKIES

1-1/2 cups sugar
1-1/2 cups brown sugar, firmly packed
2 cups margarine
4 eggs
2 t imitation vanilla
6 cups flour
1/2 t salt
2 t baking soda
1 pkg or 12-oz carob chips

Cream the sugars in the margarine. Add eggs and imitation vanilla. Stir. Add sifted dry ingredients. Stir and add the carob morsels. Drop by teaspoonfuls on cookie sheet. Bake at 325° for about 10 minutes, or until they are very brown.

PRUNE WHIP

---

1 cup sweetened, thick cooked prune puree

5 egg whites (whip until stiff, not dry)

1/4 t cream of tartar (to be added to eggs)

1 t grated lemon rind

Fold the pureed prunes into the egg white mixture. Add the lemon rind. Bake the soufflé in a baking dish set in a pan of hot water. Bake at 350° for 1 hour until firm. Serve hot with custard sauce.

CUSTARD SAUCE

1/2 cup unsalted butter

1 cup sugar

4 egg yolks

1 cup scalded milk

1-1/2 t vanilla

1 t nutmeg

Cream the unsalted butter; gradually add the sugar, beating until fluffy. Beat in, one at a time, four egg yolks. In a double boiler, heat the scalded milk, the vanilla and the nutmeg. Add to the egg mixture. Pour over hot prune whip.

RHUBARB CRUNCH

Topping

1 cup sifted flour
1/2 cup oatmeal
1 cup brown sugar
1/2 cup melted butter

Combine the ingredients to make a crumbly mixture.

Filling

4 cups rhubarb, skinned and sliced into 1-inch pieces
1 cup granulated sugar
1/4 cup flour
1/2 t cinnamon

Mix the rhubarb, sugar, flour and cinnamon in a large bowl. Spread in an 8 x 8 x 2" baking dish. Sprinkle topping over filling. Bake uncovered for 35 minutes in a 350° oven. Serve hot with yogurt.

RUSSIAN CREAM

1-1/2 cups water

1 envelope unflavored gelatin

3/4 cup sugar

1 cup plain yogurt

1-1/2 t vanilla flavoring

1 cup Dream Whip, prepared according to package directions

Combine water, gelatin and sugar. Heat, stirring until dissolved. Remove from heat. Mix yogurt and vanilla; add slowly to heated mixture. Place in refrigerator to thicken, approximately 2 hours. Fold in Dream Whip. Chill till ready to serve. Spoon into individual dessert dishes and top with your favorite fresh fruit or berries. For festive occasions, chill in a 4-cup mold, turn out onto a serving plate and top with fruit.

STRAWBERRY SHORTCAKE WITH FRESH STRAWBERRIES

Biscuits are not good for your diet because of the baking soda content so we suggest using our basic white cake recipe.

2-1/2 cups sifted cake flour
5 egg whites
1-1/2 cups sugar
3/4 cup shortening
1-1/2 t vanilla
1 T baking powder
1 cup milk

Grease and flour cake pan. Beat egg whites till stiff. Set them aside. Cream sugar, shortening and vanilla. Sift together the flour and baking powder. Combine dry ingredients with creamed mixture alternately with the milk. Gently fold in egg whites and pour into prepared cake pan. Bake in 375° oven for 18 to 20 minutes.

Clean and slice your strawberries and top warm cake with them. Top the strawberries with vanilla yogurt.

NEVER-FAIL PIE CRUST

3 cups flour
1/2 t baking powder
scant salt
1-1/4 cups Crisco shortening
1 egg, beaten
5 T ice water
1 T vinegar

Mix together the dry ingredients. Then cut in shortening. Mix together the egg, water and vinegar. Add this to the first mixture. Roll out on a floured surface. This should make 3 or 4 nice-sized pie crusts.

SALAD OIL PIE CRUST

2-1/1 cups all-purpose flour
1/2 t salt
2/3 cup salad oil
1/2 to 5/8 cup milk

Combine the flour and salt in a mixing bowl and set aside. In a measuring cup, blend together the salad oil and the milk. (I usually add about 5/8 cup. This pie crust dough is more moist than most.) Mix the liquid into the dry ingredients with a fork, just barely mixing so that there is a marbling effect. Roll out between two sheets of waxed paper. Handle as little as possible. Bake single crust at 425° for 10 minutes. Turn heat down to 375° and bake until done. For double crust, especially fruit pies, bake at 450° for 15 minutes, then turn down to 375° and bake until crust is golden brown. This recipe has never failed.

BASIC PIE CRUST

4 cups flour
1 t baking powder
dash of salt
1 T sugar
1-3/4 cup Crisco shortening
1/2 cup ice water
1 egg, beaten

Sift together the first four ingredients, then cut in the shortening and set aside. Combine the ice water and the egg. Add this to the above mixture. Roll this out on a floured surface and gently press into pie pan. If pastry is to be baked without a filling, prick bottom and sides with a fork. This helps keep the crust from puffing up. Do not prick if filling is to be baked along with the crust. Berry fillings are usually baked with the crust.

APPLE PIE

Salad oil pie crust

2-1/2 cups all-purpose flour
2/3 cup salad oil
5/8 cup milk

In a mixing bowl, combine the oil and milk, then add the flour. Barely mix so that there is a marbling effect. Roll out between two sheets of waxed paper. Handle as little as possible. Bake single crust at 425° for 10 minutes; turn heat down to 375° and bake until done. For double crusts, especially for fruit pies, bake at 450° for 15 minutes, turn heat down and bake at 375° until crust is golden brown.

Apple pie filling

2 lbs sliced apples
1 T lemon juice
1 cup sugar
2 T all-purpose flour
1 t ground cinnamon
2 T butter

Peel and core apples. Thinly slice them. Sprinkle with lemon juice. Combine sugar, flour and cinnamon. Mix with apples. Fill the pastry and dot with butter. Adjust top crust and brush with milk. Sprinkle top with sugar. Cover edges with foil. Bake at 350° for 25 minutes; remove foil and bake for 25 more minutes.

LEMON CAKE PIE

1/4 cup butter
1-1/4 cup sugar
3 T flour
1-1/2 cups milk
3 eggs, separated
juice and rind of 1 lemon

Cream the butter and the sugar together and then add flour and blend this well. Add lemon rind and juice. In a separate bowl, beat the egg yolks slightly. Add milk and combine with the creamed mixture. Beat egg whites until stiff, and fold into the mixture. Pour into an unbaked 9" pie shell. Bake at 400° for 10 minutes. Then reduce heat to 325° and bake for 25 minutes longer.

LEMON PARTY PIE

1 pkg lemon pudding and pie filling
2/3 cup sugar
1/4 cup water
3 egg yolks
2 cups water
2 T lemon juice
2 T butter
3 egg whites
1/4 t cream of tartar
6 T sugar
1 9" baked pie shell

Mix in saucepan the first 5 ingredients. Cook to a full boil, stirring constantly. Cool for 5 minutes and then blend in the lemon juice and butter. Pour into a 9" pie shell. Prepare the meringue by whipping the egg whites with the cream of tartar. Beat until frothy. Gradually add the 6 T of sugar. Beat until stiff. Top the pie with the meringue. Bake this at 425° for 5 to 10 minutes or until the meringue is golden brown.

LEMONADE PIE

6 oz frozen lemonade
4-1/2 oz pkg Dream Whip, prepared as on box
1 can sweetened condensed milk
1 t vanilla
dash salt

Blend all the ingredients together and pour into either a graham cracker crust or one of the pie crust recipes given in this book. Refrigerate this for several hours.

Because some dairy products are a maybe and milk is one of them when not cooked, we are unsure about whether or not condensed milk would be recommended for migraine patients. So we would like you to try this. However, we would like you to be aware of the possibility of getting a headache, so we are giving it a maybe on our list.

MACADAMIA NUT PIE FILLING

(Because this is the only nut on our food list that can possibly be used, we are giving you this recipe.)

3 eggs
2/3 cup sugar
1 cup white corn syrup
3 T unsalted melted butter
1 t imitation vanilla
1-1/2 cups macadamia nuts (salt rinsed off)

Combine all of the ingredients except the nuts, and beat thoroughly. Stir in the nuts, pour into a 9" pie shell and bake at 350° for 45 minutes or until filling is set. Serve warm with Dream Whip.

MACADAMIA CREAM PIE

---

1 envelope unflavored gelatin

1/4 cup sugar

2 eggs, separated

1-3/4 cup milk

1/2 t imitation vanilla

3/4 cup macadamia nuts, finely ground (a maybe on our list)

1/3 cup sugar

1 cup Dream Whip

1 baked 9" or 10" pie shell, cooked

Mix the gelatin and sugar together thoroughly in the top of a double boiler or in a heavy saucepan. Beat together the egg yolks and milk and add gelatin mixture. Cook over boiling water or on medium heat, stirring constantly until the gelatin is thoroughly dissolved. (This takes about 8 minutes.) Remove this from the heat and add vanilla. Chill to unbeaten egg white consistency. Add macadamia nuts. Beat the egg whites until stiff and beat in 1/3 cup sugar gradually. Fold in the gelatin mixture and fold in the Dream Whip; turn into pie shell and chill 12 hours before serving. Top with more crushed macadamia nuts or Dream Whip. This is out of this world!

SHOOFLY PIE

1-1/2 cups sifted flour
1/2 cup sugar
1/2 t cinnamon
1/4 t ginger
1/2 t nutmeg
1/4 cup butter
1/2 t baking soda
1/2 cup molasses
3/4 cup boiling water
1 unbaked 8" pastry shell

Mix together the flour, sugar, cinnamon, ginger and nutmeg. Cut in butter until mixture resembles coarse meal. Mix together baking soda and molasses and immediately stir in the boiling water. Stir in 1-1/3 cups of the crumb mixture and turn into pastry shell. Sprinkle the remaining 2/3 cup of the crumb mixture over the top and bake at 375° for 30 to 40 minutes until the crust is slightly brown.

BREAD PUDDING

3/4 cup sugar
6 eggs, beaten
4-1/2 cups milk
1 t imitation vanilla
1 loaf bread, cubed (homemade is really good)
1/2 cup seedless raisins
3 T milk
3 T butter

Add beaten eggs to the sugar in a large bowl. Slowly stir in the milk and vanilla and add the bread, raisins, milk and butter. Stir well. Pour into a 9" square baking pan and place on a rack, a little below the center of the oven for even baking temperature. Bake at 350° for about 1 hour or until knife inserted near the center comes out clean. It is real easy and pretty good!

SIMPLE BREAD PUDDING
AN OLD FAMILY TRADITION

1 stick butter
4 pieces bread, toasted
2 cups milk
3 eggs
1 cup sugar
cinnamon
nutmeg

Melt butter in a 6 x 12 inch dish. Toast bread until brown on both sides. Break into rather large pieces in the dish. Scald the milk (very important to do this since it is the only way the migraine sufferer can use milk) and add to eggs beaten with sugar. Add this mixture to toast and butter in dish. Sprinkle generously with cinnamon and nutmeg. Put dish in a pan of boiling water and bake for 35 minutes at 350°. When a knife inserted comes out clean, remove from oven.

PAPAYA PUDDING

1/4 cup butter
1/2 cup sugar
1 egg, beaten
1 cup flour
2 cups ripe papaya pulp, mashed (about 2 medium-size papayas)
1/2 cup bread crumbs
1 t imitation vanilla

Cream the butter and sugar and add the well-beaten egg and flour. Add the papaya, bread crumbs and vanilla, and steam in a buttered pan for 2-1/2 hours or until done. Serve with sauce. (Recipe on next page.)

SAUCE FOR PAPAYA PUDDING

1 cup milk
1/2 cup ripe papaya pulp
1/3 cup sugar
2 T flour
1/4 t imitation vanilla

Mix all the ingredients except the flavoring, and boil continuously until thick. Then add the flavoring immediately after you remove from the heat. While this is still warm, pour it over the papaya pudding.

RAW APPLE ICING

1 raw apple, sliced
1 cup sugar
1 egg white
juice of 1/2 lemon

Put all of the ingredients in a bowl and beat, starting on low speed and increasing speed until mixture is thick enough to spread. This icing is ideal for spice cake, pound cake, or your favorite boxed cake mix.

BROWN SUGAR ICING

1 cup brown sugar
1 egg white
2 T boiling water

Boil sugar and water for 2-1/2 minutes after it begins to bubble vigorously. Beat egg white stiff. Pour syrup over egg white and beat until ready to spread. This icing is great over any kind of spice, apple or banana cake.

DIVINITY FROSTING

1 cup sugar
3/4 cup water
2 egg whites
1/8 t cream of tartar
1 t vanilla
powdered sugar

Boil sugar and water until it threads. Pour slowly into egg whites that have been beaten with cream of tartar. (Use electric beater, if possible.) Beat continuously while pouring in cooked mixture. Add vanilla. For decorating cakes, stir in enough powdered sugar to make stiff. This is very good on carob cake.

FRUIT GLAZE FOR ANGEL FOOD CAKE

1/4 cup frozen orange juice concentrate
1/4 cup strained baby food (applesauce and apricots)
1/2 cup brown sugar
1/4 cup butter or margarine

In a saucepan, combine undiluted orange juice concentrate, strained baby food, sugar and butter. Stir over low heat to blend. Boil 5 minutes. Cool and brush on outside of cake.

REFRIGERATOR FROSTING

1-1/2 cup milk minus 2 T
1 small pkg instant lemon pudding
1 pkg Dream Whip

Scald the milk, then let it cool to room temperature. Put all ingredients together in large bowl. Whip at high speed until light. This frosts an 8" layer cake. Double this recipe and it will generously frost a large angel food cake. If you wish to change the flavoring from lemon, you may choose another instant pudding to comply with your recipe.

NOTE: After frosting the cake, it must be kept cool in the refrigerator.

SEVEN-MINUTE WHITE FROSTING

2 unbeaten egg whites
1-1/2 cups sugar
5 T cold water
1/4 t cream of tartar
1-1/2 t light corn syrup
1 t vanilla flavoring

Combine all ingredients except vanilla in the top of a double boiler. Cook over rapidly boiling water for 7 minutes, beating constantly. Remove from heat and add vanilla. Continue beating until correct consistency to spread. This makes enough icing for a two-layer cake.

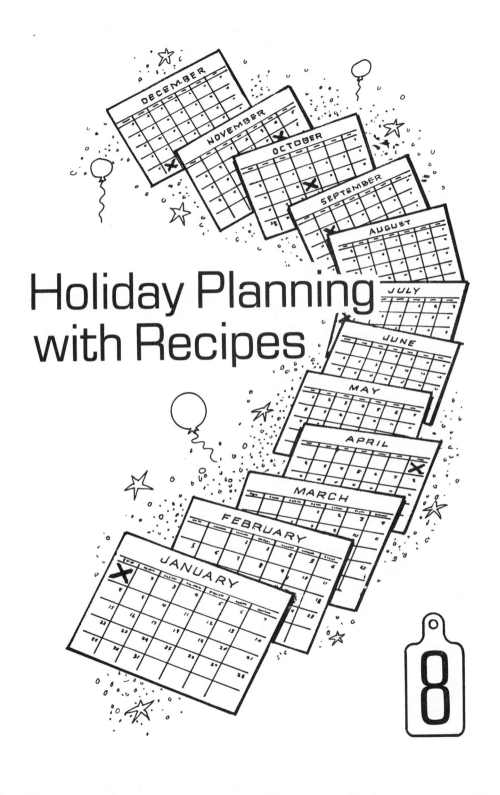

Holiday Planning
with Recipes

8

HOLIDAY PLANNING WITH RECIPES

There is little question that holidays create a special problem for the migraine patient. In addition to the stress frequently associated with this particular time, our foods are frequently laced with triggering agents. In planning the holiday menu, our main goal was to show you that these meals could be enjoyed with little problem. You will notice we have touched on favorite dishes from most parts of the world. We hope to have touched on the interest of almost everyone in our society. Again, we wish to emphasize that you may be creative, substituting your favorite dishes. Remember, however, to refer back to your food list and introduce changes slowly to eliminate the troublesome ingredients. Here, again, I wish to encourage you to venture out into the "maybe" food group, using discretion and looking upon it as a challenge in your new diet.

We have especially enjoyed this particular part of our book because it enabled us to include some of our favorite dishes, allowing us to experiment with the substitutes. In some cases we found the taste of that particular dish to be better and the substitute better for us. It was a challenge pleasing the holiday palate not only for ourselves but also for our families and friends.

Holiday Menus

JANUARY—NEW YEAR'S EVE BUFFET:

Vegetable Nibbles with Dill Dip

Shrimp Spread on Miniature Bagels

Northwest Oyster Stew

All-American White Bread

Hush Puppies

Festive Jelly Roll

Lemon Bars

Grandma's Favorite Apple Bundt Cake

Coffee

JANUARY—SUPER BOWL SUNDAY:

Barbecued Spare Ribs

Mini Drum Sticks

Sesame Puffs

Western Salad

Crockpot Chili

Basic Spoon Bread

Gingerbread

Frosted Orange Drops

Hot Apple Cider

Spiced Peach Punch Delight

Coffee

FEBRUARY—VALENTINE SWEETHEART DINNER:

Cranberry Vodka Fizz

Marinated Beef Burgundy Tips/Noodles or Rice

Stuffed Avocado and Crab Salad

Croissants

Strawberry Sweetheart Cake

FEBRUARY—CHINESE NEW YEAR'S DINNER:

Egg Drop Soup

Mandarin Orange Salad

Chinese Pepper Steak

Sweet-and-Sour Chicken

Brown Rice

Oriental Ginger Fruit

MARCH—ST. PATRICK'S DAY:

Combination Green Salad with Green Goddess Dressing

Irish Stew

Boiled Potatoes

Cottage Cheese Bread

Kiwi Cream Pie

Irish Coffee

MARCH—PASSOVER SEDER:

White Fish and Pike with Horseradish

Hot Borscht or Chicken Soup with Fluffy Matzo Balls

Honeyed Duck with Orange Sauce

Broccoli with Velvet Sauce

Carrot and Raisin Salad

Matzos

Dilled Tomatoes

Chiffon Cake with Spicy Fruit Sauce

Lemon Meringue Pie

Tea, Black Coffee

APRIL—EASTER DINNER:

Cucumber Vinaigrette Salad

Honey-Glazed Game Hens

Wild Rice Pilaf

Acorn Squash Cups with Peas

Potato Bread

Angel Food Cake

MAY—CINCO DE MAYO, A MEXICAN FIESTA:

Gazpacho

Guacamole Salad with Shrimp and Chips

Tostadas

Spanish Rice

Flan

MAY—MOTHER'S DAY BRUNCH:

Vichyssoise (Cold Potato Soup)

Sweet Ambrosia

Chicken Cream Crepes

Cold Lemon Soufflé

JUNE—ENJOYING THE CULINARY ART OF GREECE:

Stuffed Grape Leaves

Lemon Egg Soup

A La "Grecque" Salad with Spinach Yogurt Dressing

Moussaka

Meatballs with Avgolemona Sauce

Baklava

JULY—INDEPENDENCE DAY PICNIC GOODIES:

Fresh Vegetable Tray with Corky's Dill Dip

Macaroni Salad

Jello/Fruit Mold

Chicken Bar-B-Que

Scalloped Potatoes

Cookies

Watermelon

Apple Punch Delight—A Southern Treat

AUGUST—ITALIAN CUISINE:

Antipasto

Tomato-Garlic Vegetable Soup

Pork Chops Italiano

Pasta Side Dish

Fresh Asparagus Sauté

Strawberry Water Ice

Crostata

SEPTEMBER—MOTHER'S BACK TO SCHOOL LUNCH:

Chilled Tomato Soup

Crepes

Chinese Salad

Date-Filled Sugar Cookies

OCTOBER—OCTOBER FEST:

Cream of Mushroom Soup

Three Bean Salad

German Potato Salad

Crock Pot Sauerbraten

Cabbage with Onion and Apple

Pumpernickel Rye Bread

Apple Streusel

Pumpkin Cookies

OCTOBER—ADULT HALLOWEEN PARTY:

Hot Apple Cider
Cranberry Bread
Apple Dumplings
Crunchies

NOVEMBER—THANKSGIVING:

Herbed Spinach Soup
Cranberry Molded Salad
Roast Turkey with Bread Stuffing
Jan's Grandmother's Cranberry Pudding
Mashed Potatoes and Gravy
Your Favorite Vegetables
Sweet Potatoes with Apple Rings
Pumpkin Pie

DECEMBER—CHRISTMAS EVE SUPPER:

Cajun Shrimp Stew
Corn Bread
Avocado and Artichoke Salad
Christmas Cookies

DECEMBER—CHRISTMAS DINNER:

Roast Beef
Yorkshire Pudding
Mashed Potatoes and Gravy
Green Beans with Basil
Cranberry Sauce Relish
Mincemeat Turnovers
Holiday Jewel

JANUARY—NEW YEAR'S EVE BUFFET:

Hors D'oeuvres
Vegetable Nibbles (plain or marinated) and Dill Dip
Shrimp Spread and Miniature Bagels

Entree
Northwest Oyster Stew

Breads and Cakes
All-American White Batter Bread

Hush Puppies

Festive Jelly Roll

Lemon Bars

Grandma's Favorite Apple Bundt Cake

VEGETABLE NIBBLES
(Plain or marinated—cook's choice)

mushrooms, whole, small
artichoke hearts
broccoli flowerets
cauliflower flowerets
celery, 1-inch pieces
small green onions
carrot rounds

Clean all of the vegetables and cut them into bite-size pieces.

DILL DIP

1 cup sour cream
1/2 cup Miracle Whip salad dressing
2 T dill seasoning
1 t onion seasoning
1 T lemon juice

Combine all ingredients. Mix well.

MARINADE

1/2 cup olive oil
1-1/2 cup water
1/4 cup onion flakes
2 T tarragon
2 T oregano
2 garlic pods (to be removed later)
cayenne pepper (small amount)

Combine all ingredients. Mix well. Marinate the vegetable nibbles for several hours before serving. They should be refrigerated and kept in a tightly sealed container. The vegetables are all very good marinated, and when drained are delicious with the dill dip.

SHRIMP SPREAD

1 envelope unflavored gelatin
3/4 cup cold water
1/2 cup Miracle Whip salad dressing
1/4 cup diced cucumber
1/4 cup diced green pepper
2 T lemon juice
1 t sugar
1 t prepared horseradish
1/2 t onion juice
1/4 t salt
1 8-oz cup plain yogurt
2 4-oz cans shrimp, drained

1. In saucepan, soften gelatin in the cold water; heat and stir until the gelatin is dissolved.
2. Remove from the heat and beat in the Miracle Whip salad dressing. Refrigerate and chill until this is partially set, about 1 hour.
3. Combine the cucumber, green pepper, lemon juice, sugar, horseradish, onion juice, salt and yogurt. Fold this into the gelatin mixture.
4. Fold in the shrimp. Refrigerate until you are ready to use.

MINIATURE BAGELS

Recipe found on page 83.

NORTHWEST OYSTER STEW

1-1/2 pints light or heavy cream (cream is a maybe)

1-1/2 pints oysters and their liquor

onion flakes

4 T soft butter

salt to taste

pepper, freshly ground

paprika

Tabasco (optional) to taste

---

1. In a saucepan, bring cream almost but not quite to a boil over moderate heat. When small bubbles appear around the edges of the pan, reduce the heat to its lowest point and keep the cream barely simmering.
2. Pour the oysters and all their liquor into a 12" skillet. Set it over moderate heat and poach the oysters, turning them about in their liquor. Do this for 3-5 minutes or until oysters' edges begin to curl. Add the onion flakes and butter at this point.
3. Pour the simmered cream into the skillet of oysters and onions. Add salt and pepper to taste and simmer a minute longer. Ladle the stew into heated soup bowls and sprinkle with a little paprika and a dash of Tabasco (if desired). Serve at once.

ALL-AMERICAN WHITE BATTER BREAD

3 cups warm water (110°)
2 pkg active dry yeast
4 T soft shortening (Crisco)
4 T sugar
1 T salt
6 cups all-purpose flour

1. In a mixing bowl, combine the warmed water, yeast and sugar. Set aside for about 5 minutes (long enough to let the yeast work and start to foam).
2. Add the shortening, salt and half of the flour. Beat 2 minutes on medium speed.
3. Add the remainder of the flour and blend with a spoon until smooth.
4. Cover with a cloth and let rise in a warm place until double in size, about 30 minutes.
5. Stir down by beating with a spoon, about 25 strokes. Spread evenly in Crisco shortening-greased loaf pan, 9 x 5 x 3. The batter will be sticky. Let rise about 1 inch from the top of the pan.
6. Bake in a 375° oven for 40 to 45 minutes. The top crust should sound hollow. Brush with melted butter. Makes 3 loaves, using 9 x 5 x 3" pans.

LEMON BARS

Recipe found on page 187.

GRANDMA'S FAVORITE
APPLE BUNDT CAKE

Recipe found on page 155.

HUSH PUPPIES

1 egg, beaten
1 cup buttermilk
1/2 cup finely chopped onion
1/4 cup finely chopped green pepper
1/4 cup water
1-3/4 cup cornmeal
1/2 cup all-purpose flour
2 T sugar
2 t baking powder
1 t salt
1/2 t baking soda
corn oil for deep fat frying

1. Blend egg, buttermilk, onion, pepper and water. Set aside.
2. Combine cornmeal, flour, sugar, baking powder, salt and soda.
3. Add egg mixture to cornmeal mixture and stir until moist.
4. Drop batter by tablespoonfuls into deep hot fat (375°).
5. Fry about 2 minutes or until golden brown, turning once.
6. Drain on paper towels. Serve hot with butter, if desired. Makes 24.

FESTIVE JELLY ROLL

4 egg yolks
1/3 cup sugar
1/2 t vanilla
4 egg whites
1/2 cup sugar
1/2 cup all-purpose flour
1 t baking powder
1/4 t salt
sifted powdered sugar
1/2 cup jelly or jam (preferably lemon custard or raspberry jam)

1. Beat egg yolks at high speed for about 5 minutes or until thick and lemon-colored.
2. Gradually add the 1/3 cup of sugar, beating until sugar dissolves. Add vanilla. Mix well.
3. Beat egg whites at medium speed until soft peaks form.
4. Gradually add the 1/2 cup sugar. Continue beating until stiff peaks form.
5. Fold yolks into whites.
6. Combine flour, baking powder and salt. Sprinkle over egg mixture.
7. Gently fold in flour mixture just until blended.
8. Grease and lightly flour a 15 x 10 x 1 inch jelly roll pan. Spread batter evenly in pan.
9. Bake in 375° oven for 12-15 minutes or until done.
10. Immediately loosen edges of cake from pan and turn out onto a dish towel and sprinkle with powdered sugar.
11. Starting with narrow end, roll the warm cake and towel together. Cool on wire rack.
12. Unroll. Spread cake with jelly, jam or pudding, leaving a 1" rim.
13. Roll up the cake. Make 10 slices. Chill before slicing.

JANUARY—SUPER BOWL DINNER:

Hors D'oeuvres
Barbecued Spare Ribs

Mini Drum Sticks

Sesame Puffs

Salad
Western Salad

Entree
Crock Pot Chili

Basic Spoon Bread

Dessert
Gingerbread

Frosted Orange Drops

Beverage
Hot Apple Cider

Spiced Peach Punch Delight

Coffee

BARBECUED SPARE RIBS

Recipe found on page 118.

MINI DRUM STICKS

3 lb small chicken wings (about 15)
1/2 cup granulated sugar
3 T cornstarch
1 t salt
1/2 t ground ginger
1/4 t pepper
3/4 cup water
1/3 cup lemon juice
1/4 cup soy sauce (soy sauce is a maybe)

1. Divide wings in half.
2. Place in a single layer in broiler pan and bake in oven at 400° for 15 minutes, turning once.
3. Mix sugar, cornstarch, salt, ginger and pepper in a small saucepan. Stir in water, lemon juice and soy sauce. Cook, stirring constantly until mixture thickens and boils 3 minutes. Brush part of mixture over wings.
4. Continue baking, turning and brushing several times with remaining lemon mixture, for 30 minutes or until richly glazed.
5. Serve in a chafing dish or keep hot. Serve hot.

SESAME PUFFS

2-1/4 cups sifted all-purpose flour
1/2 t garlic powder
3/4 cup butter or margarine
3/4 cup dairy sour cream (sour cream is a maybe)
sesame seeds

1. Sift flour and garlic powder. Cut in butter or margarine with a pastry blender until the mixture is crumbly.
2. Stir in sour cream lightly with a fork just until pastry holds together and leaves side of bowl clean. Wrap in waxed paper and chill overnight in the refrigerator.
3. Roll out pastry 1/4" thick on a *lightly* floured pastry cloth. Cut into rounds or fancy shapes with a floured, small cookie cutter. Place on ungreased cookie sheets. Brush cutouts with water. Sprinkle with sesame seeds.
4. Bake in hot oven (400°) 15 minutes or until puffed and golden. Remove from cookie sheets to wire racks. Cool.
5. Puffs may be made a couple of days in advance and stored in a tightly covered container so they will stay crisp. May be served hot or cold.

WESTERN SALAD

1/2 medium-size head iceberg lettuce, shredded (4 cups)
1 small red apple, halved, cored and sliced thin
1/2 small Bermuda onion, peeled and sliced thin
1/2 cup thinly sliced celery
2 medium carrots, shredded
1/2 cup sweet garlic french dressing

1. Combine lettuce, apple, onion, celery and carrots in a large salad bowl.
2. Drizzle dressing over top. Toss lightly to mix. Makes 6 servings.

BASIC SPOON BREAD

2 cups water
1 cup white cornmeal
1 t salt
4 T butter
5 eggs
1 cup milk
3/4 cup medium cream (cream is a maybe; however, cooked it should be all right)

1. Preheat oven to 350°. Heat the water to boiling in a large saucepan.
2. Add the cornmeal and the salt. Stir briskly and cook for 1 minute or until very thick.
3. Remove from heat and stir in 2 T butter.
4. Place remaining butter in a 9" square baking pan or baking dish, and put into the oven until butter is sizzling but not brown.
5. Beat in 4 of the eggs and mix in the milk. Stir egg mixture into cornmeal. Beat with electric beater until free from lumps. Take the baking pan from the oven and pour batter into it. Return to the oven and bake for 15 minutes.
6. Beat the remaining egg with the cream. Pour the egg mixture over the top of the bread and continue baking for 25 minutes or until the top is lightly browned and puffy. Spoon onto plates and serve immediately with plenty of butter. Serves 8 people.

GINGERBREAD

Recipe found on page 165.

CROCK POT CHILI

---

3 lb top round cut into 1/2" cubes

6 T vegetable oil

2 cups coarsely chopped onion

2 whole cloves garlic

2 T chili powder (adjust to taste)

1 t oregano

1 t ground cumin

1 t red pepper flakes (optional, it makes chili exceptionally hot)

1 6-oz can tomato paste

4 cups beef stock, fresh or canned

1 t salt

fresh ground pepper to taste

1-1/2 cups freshly cooked red kidney beans or drained canned kidney beans (optional)

2 cups finely chopped celery

2 cups finely chopped green pepper

---

1. In a 12" heavy skillet, heat 4 T oil and cook meat on high for 2-3 minutes, stirring until the meat is lightly browned. Break up the cubes into shreds as you brown it.
2. Add the remaining 2 T of oil to the skillet, and in it cook the onion, garlic cloves, celery and green pepper for 4 to 5 minutes, stirring frequently.
3. Remove the skillet from the heat. Add the 2 T chili powder (or to taste), oregano, cumin and pepper flakes, and stir until the onions are well coated with the mixture.
4. Add the tomato paste, beef stock, salt and pepper. If you are using the beans, add them to the chili mixture when you add the tomato paste. Bring to a boil, stirring once or twice, then half cover the pot, turning the heat to simmer. Let cook for 1 to 1-1/2 hours or until the meat is tender.

5. When using a crock pot, follow the above recipe through #3. Now place the browned meat into your crock pot and add the ingredients as in #4. Let cook all day or until the meat is tender.

FROSTED ORANGE DROPS

Recipe found on page 182.

HOT APPLE CIDER

Recipe found on page 328.

SPICED PEACH PUNCH DELIGHT

1 46-oz can peach nectar
1 20-oz can orange juice
1/2 cup firmly packed brown sugar (brown sugar is a maybe)
3 three-inch pieces of stick cinnamon, broken
1/2 t whole cloves
2 T bottled lime juice
1 bottle ginger ale (use only if served cold)

1. Combine peach nectar, orange juice and brown sugar in a saucepan. Tie cinnamon and cloves in a small cheesecloth bag. Drop into saucepan.
2. Heat slowly, stirring constantly until sugar dissolves. Simmer 10 minutes. Stir in lime juice. If serving cold, add the ginger ale.
3. Serve either hot or cold in mugs. Garnish with cinnamon and orange peel.

FEBRUARY—VALENTINE SWEETHEART DINNER

Entree
Marinated Beef Burgundy Tips over Noodles or Rice

Salad
Stuffed Avocado and Crab Salad

Bread
Croissants

Dessert
Strawberry Sweetheart Cake

Beverage
Cranberry Vodka Fizz

MARINATED BEEF BURGUNDY TIPS OVER NOODLES OR RICE

---

18 small onions, peeled, or 4 medium onions, peeled and quartered

4 T butter

1 lb fresh mushrooms, sliced in half

3 lbs lean boneless beef rump, cut into 2" chunks

2 T finely chopped shallots

1/4 cup finely chopped carrots

3 T flour

1 cup hot beef stock, fresh or canned (fresh is less salty and we prefer it)

2 cups red burgundy

1 T tomato paste

1 t finely chopped garlic

1 t thyme

1 t salt

cracked black pepper

2 T parsley, finely chopped (for garnish)

---

1. Preheat oven to 350°.
2. Sauté onions in 2 T butter until brown but still firm. Transfer onions to a shallow baking disk large enough to hold them in 1 layer. Bake the onions uncovered for 30 minutes or until they are barely tender. Remove them from the oven and set aside.
3. Sauté mushrooms in 1 T butter for 2 or 3 minutes until they are slightly soft. Add to the onions and set aside.
4. Quickly brown the meat on all sides over high heat. This must be given your constant attention. Do not let the cubes of meat burn. Fast browning helps tenderize the meat. When browned, place in a heavy 4-6 quart casserole.

5. Brown the chopped shallots and finely chopped carrots in a skillet with 1 T of butter, and cook over low heat until they are lightly colored. Stir in the flour and cook, stirring constantly until the flour begins to brown lightly. This must have your constant attention. Remove from heat and let cool a minute. Pour in the beef stock, beating vigorously with a wire whisk. Blend in the wine and tomato paste and bring to a boil, whisking constantly as the sauce thickens.

6. Blend your spices (except parsley) together and then sprinkle them in the sauce. Pour sauce over beef and toss gently to moisten. Add more wine or beef stock if sauce does not almost cover meat. Bake in lower oven 2 to 3 hours or until meat is fork tender. Stir the onions, mushrooms and their juices into the beef mixture in casserole an hour before the casserole is scheduled to be done.

7. This may be prepared the day before and reheated before serving. To serve, skim the fat and taste for seasonings. Sprinkle with parsley and serve on top of noodles or rice.

STUFFED AVOCADO AND CRAB SALAD

---

1 lb crab legs, cooked, chilled and shelled (1/2 lb crab meat) or 1 7-oz can crab meat, chilled and drained

---

2 hard-boiled eggs, chopped

1/4 cup chopped celery

1/4 cup mayonnaise or salad dressing

---

1 t dry mustard

1/4 t salt

---

dash of Worcestershire sauce (this is a maybe for some users)

---

4 medium avocados

---

1. Break crab meat into pieces. Set aside several larger segments of meat. Combine remaining crab meat with eggs, celery, mayonnaise or salad dressing, mustard, salt and Worcestershire sauce. Chill. (Worchestershire sauce is a maybe.)
2. Prepare avocado shells by cutting each avocado in half. Remove the pit and peel the skin off the avocado, leaving the fruit intact.
3. Fill the avocados with the crab mixture. Top with pieces of reserved crab meat. Serve on lettuce-lined plates, if desired. One serving consists of one stuffed avocado half. This recipe makes 8 servings.

STRAWBERRY SWEETHEART CAKE

Recipe found on page 172.

CRANBERRY VODKA FIZZ

1 part club soda
1 part cranberry juice
1 lime wedge

Combine the ingredients and serve over crushed ice. If vodka does not affect you, you may add 1/2 jigger per 8-oz glass or to taste.

CROISSANTS

1-1/2 cups butter

1/3 cup all-purpose flour

---

2 pkg active dry yeast

1/2 cup warm water (110°-115°). (The temperature of the water is very important as it will kill the yeast if it is too hot.)

3-3/4 to 4-1/4 cups all-purpose flour

3/4 cup milk

1/4 cup sugar

---

1 t salt (Do not add the salt to the yeast. Add it to the flour because salt may kill the yeast.)

---

1 egg

---

1 egg yolk

---

1 T milk

---

1. Cream the butter with the 1/3 cup flour.
2. Roll into a 12 x 6 inch rectangle and chill.
3. Sprinkle yeast over warm water and stir to dissolve. Combine 1-1/2 cups of flour and the yeast/water.
4. Heat milk, sugar and 1 t salt until warm (115°-120°).
5. Add to the flour mixture and add the egg.
6. Beat at low speed for 1/2 minute. Beat 3 minutes at high speed.
7. Stir in enough of the remaining flour to make soft dough.
8. Turn out onto floured surface. Knead about 5 minutes.
9. Let rest 10 minutes.
10. Roll into a 14" square.
11. Place chilled butter mixture on half of the dough. Fold over other half of dough and seal.
12. Roll into a rectangle (approximately 21" x 12").
13. Fold into thirds. Roll again into rectangle.
14. Repeat, folding and rolling two more times. Chill after each rolling. (The butter between the layers and the constant folding and rolling are what make the croissants light and flaky.)

15. Fold into thirds 12" x 7". Chill several hours or overnight.
16. Cut dough crosswise in fourths. Roll each fourth into a 12" circle. Cut each into 12 wedges. Roll each wedge loosely, starting from wide edge. Roll toward point. Place point down, 2 to 3" apart on ungreased baking sheet.
17. Let rise on baking sheet, covered, 30 to 45 minutes.
18. Beat egg yolk and 1 T milk. Brush on rolls. Bake at 375° for 12 to 15 minutes. Remove from baking sheet. Makes 48 dinner-size croissants.

FEBRUARY—CHINESE NEW YEAR'S:

Soup
Egg Drop Soup

Salad
Mandarin Orange Salad

Entree
Chinese Pepper Steak

Sweet-and-Sour Chicken

Brown Rice

Dessert
Oriental Ginger Fruit

EGG DROP SOUP

3 cups homemade chicken stock
1 T cornstarch
2 T cold chicken stock or cold water
2 or 3 thinly sliced mushrooms (optional)
1 egg, lightly beaten
1 green onion, finely chopped, including top

1. To make homemade chicken stock, place chicken pieces such as backs in a heavy stock pan. Cover with water. Add 1 celery rib chopped into 3 or 4 pieces and 1/4 of a large onion stuck with 2 whole cloves. Bring water to a boil, lower heat and simmer, covered, for 25 to 30 minutes. Remove vegetables and chicken, skim fat, and use remaining stock for soup base. Can be made a day or two ahead and kept in refrigerator.
2. Bring chicken stock to a boil over high heat in a 2-quart saucepan. Dissolve cornstarch in cold chicken stock or cold water; stir while adding to boiling stock. Continue to stir for a few minutes, until the mixture clears and thickens. Add mushrooms, if using. Slowly pour in egg, stir, and turn off heat. Serve topped with chopped onions.

MANDARIN ORANGE SALAD

1 lb spinach greens, cleaned and torn into pieces
1/2 cup cleaned bean sprouts (optional)
1 5-oz can sliced water chestnuts (drained)
1 10-oz can mandarin oranges, drained (save juice)
chow mein noodles (for garnish)
2 thinly sliced green onions

1. Toss greens and sprouts. Add water chestnuts and mandarin oranges.
2. Dress with homemade french dressing (recipe in this cookbook) in which orange juice has been substituted for lemon juice. (Rice vinegar may be substituted for cider vinegar.)
3. Garnish with chow mein noodles and onion slices.

CHINESE PEPPER STEAK

1-1/2 lb round steak
2 T vegetable oil
1 medium onion, chopped
1 clove garlic, minced (optional)
2 green peppers, diced
1 cup low-salt beef bouillon
1 cup skinned, seeded tomatoes, chopped
1-1/2 T cornstarch
1/4 cup cold water
1 T soy sauce

1. Cut steak into thin strips, 1/8 inch wide by 1 inch long.
2. Brown in hot oil over medium heat.
3. Season with pepper if desired, add onion and garlic, and cook until onion begins to wilt.
4. Add peppers and bouillon, cover, and simmer for 10 minutes.
5. Add tomatoes; simmer, covered, for 5 minutes.
6. Mix cornstarch, water and soy sauce. Add, stirring constantly until mixture thickens.
7. Serve over rice.

SWEET-AND-SOUR CHICKEN

Recipe found on page 95.

BROWN RICE

1/2 cup finely diced chicken
2 T salad oil
1 3-oz can broiled sliced mushrooms, drained
4 cups chilled, day-old, cooked long-grain rice
1 green onion, finely chopped
1 small green pepper, finely chopped
1 T soy sauce (This is a maybe. Too salty for most people.)
1 well-beaten egg

1. Brown the meat in the oil in a skillet or wok.
2. Add the mushrooms, rice, onion, pepper and soy sauce.
3. Fry over low heat for 10 minutes, stirring frequently.
4. Add the well-beaten egg and continue to stir-fry for another 5 minutes, or until dry enough to be fluffy. Makes 6-8 servings.

ORIENTAL GINGER FRUIT

1 1-lb can sliced peaches, drained
1 cup orange juice
1 can mandarin oranges, drained
2 t finely chopped candied ginger
2 bananas, sliced
1 cup halved kumquats

1. Mix all of the above in a bowl.
2. Refrigerate for several hours.
3. Serve in individual bowls and garnish with a sprig of mint.

MARCH—ST. PATRICK'S DAY:

Salad
Combination Green Salad with Green Goddess Dressing

Entree
Irish Stew

Boiled Potatoes

Bread
Cottage Cheese Bread

Dessert
Kiwi Cream Pie

Beverage
Irish Coffee without the Irish if you cannot use the alcohol. If whiskey is a maybe, you may try a taste in your coffee. A suggestion would be Jameson's Irish Whiskey.

COMBINATION GREEN SALAD

1/2 head iceberg lettuce, cleaned, torn in bite-size pieces and dried

---

2 medium tomatoes, cleaned, cored and chopped

1/4 medium Bermuda onion, sliced thin

---

1 medium cucumber, peeled and sliced thin

1/4 medium green pepper, cleaned and chopped

1/2 cup mushrooms, cleaned and sliced

1/4 cup radishes, cleaned and sliced

---

2 hard-boiled eggs, sliced

---

1 cup croutons (french bread buttered, toasted and cubed)

In a large bowl, prepare and combine the above vegetables in the order given. Cover and refrigerate until you are ready to serve. Just before you serve, garnish with commercial Green Goddess dressing and the croutons.

IRISH STEW

2 lb breast of lamb, cut in 1" cubes
1 cup carrots (chopped very fine)
2 T butter
1 cup hot water
salt and pepper to taste
1 cup milk
1/2 cup cream for gravy (more milk if needed)
flour
1/2 t ground ginger

1. Brown cubed meat and 1 cup chopped carrots in 2 T butter. Add 1 cup of hot water and 1/2 t salt and a dash of pepper.
2. Cover and cook for 45 minutes to an hour, or until almost done.
3. Add 1 cup milk and 1/2 cup thin cream for gravy. Continue to simmer over low heat, stirring occasionally to avoid scorching milk and cream.
4. Thicken with flour stirred into water and flavor with ginger.

COTTAGE CHEESE BREAD

3/4 cup softened butter
1 pint small curd cottage cheese
1/8 t salt
2 cups flour
poppy seeds (for garnish)

1. Blend the butter, cottage cheese, salt and flour with a mixer until smooth.
2. Divide dough into 4 parts. Roll each on floured board to 9" round.
3. Sprinkle lightly with poppy seeds.
4. Cut into 8 wedges. Roll wide end to narrow and curve into crescents. Bake at 400° for 20-25 minutes or until golden brown.

KIWI CREAM PIE

6 T cake flour
2/3 cup sugar
1/4 t salt
1-3/4 cups milk
2 egg yolks, slightly beaten
1-1/4 t imitation vanilla
1/2 cup Dream Whip
7 kiwi
1/2 lemon
1 baked 9" pie shell
whipped cream (Whipped cream is a maybe. Dream Whip may be substituted.)
1 T grated orange rind

1. Mix together flour, sugar and salt in the top of a double boiler.
2. Add milk and cook over hot water, stirring constantly until mixture thickens. Cook 15 minutes longer, stirring occasionally.
3. Pour small amount of mixture over egg yolks, beating vigorously. Return to double boiler and cook 2 minutes longer, stirring constantly. Remove from heat. Cool. Add vanilla. Chill. Fold in Dream Whip. Layer cream filling and sliced kiwi. Sprinkle the kiwi with lemon juice after placing in the pie shell.
4. Garnish with kiwi slices and whipped cream.
5. Sprinkle with the grated orange rind.

IRISH COFFEE

Good, hot black coffee with a jigger of Jameson's Irish Whiskey. You may try this if alcohol does not bother you. Do not overdo.

MARCH—PASSOVER SEDER:

Appetizer
White Fish and Pike with Horseradish

Soup
Borscht

Chicken Soup with Fluffy Matzo Balls

Salad
Carrot and Raisin Salad

Entree
Honeyed Duck with Orange Sauce

Vegetable
Broccoli with Velvet Sauce

Dilled Tomatoes

Bread
Matzos

Dessert
Chiffon Cake with Spicy Fruit Sauce

Lemon Meringue Pie

WHITE FISH AND PIKE WITH HORSERADISH

These are prepared foods which can be bought in specialty sections of grocery stores and Jewish delicatessens. Matzos can be bought there as well.

BORSCHT

1 cup finely chopped onion
2 cups finely chopped beets
1 clove minced garlic
1 T butter
2 cups chicken stock
1 T vinegar

1. Barely cover first 3 ingredients with water in pan. Cover pan and simmer for 15 minutes.
2. Add remaining ingredients and simmer for 15 more minutes. May be mixed in blender if not smooth enough.
3. Place in soup bowls and serve. Non-migraines' servings may be topped with 1 T sour cream.

CHICKEN SOUP WITH FLUFFY MATZO BALLS

---

3 qt chicken soup (recipe in this cookbook)

3 eggs, separated

very slight dash of salt

3/4 cup matzo meal

2 T parsley

pepper

---

1. Prepare the homemade chicken soup, and set aside while you make the matzo balls.
2. Beat egg whites until stiff.
3. Beat egg yolks with the dash of salt. Fold in egg whites.
4. Fold in matzo meal and parsley. Sprinkle with pepper. Let stand for 5 minutes.
5. Form into 12 large balls and drop into boiling stock. Cover and cook for 35 minutes.

CARROT AND RAISIN SALAD

---

3 cups grated raw carrots

1/4 cup raisins

lemon juice and mayonnaise to moisten

---

1. Combine all ingredients.
2. Chill and serve on lettuce.

HONEYED DUCK WITH ORANGE SAUCE

2 large ducks (reserve giblets and necks)
1/2 cup honey
2 t paprika

1. Roast ducks for 2-1/2 hours at 350°. Turn to brown evenly.
2. Mix honey with paprika. Brush all sides of duck with half of the mixture. Turn after 15 minutes and brush with remaining mixture.
3. Bake until skin is crisp, about 15 minutes longer.
4. Serve with orange sauce. (Recipe follows.)

ORANGE SAUCE

giblets and necks from 2 ducks
1-1/2 cups chicken soup
2 T potato starch
3/4 cup orange juice
dash ginger
1/4 cup honey
2 t grated orange rind

1. Cook giblets and necks in soup until tender. Strain and save 3/4 cup of stock.
2. Mix potato starch with a little orange juice. Add remaining orange juice and ginger. Add stock, honey and orange rind.
3. Cook over low heat, stirring constantly until thickened.
4. Serve immediately.

BROCCOLI WITH VELVET SAUCE

1 bunch broccoli, trimmed
1/4 cup chicken soup
2 t finely minced onion
1 cup mayonnaise
1/2 t lemon juice

1. Cook broccoli. Set aside.
2. Bring soup and onion to a boil.
3. Remove from heat and add mayonnaise gradually, stirring constantly.
4. Cook over a double boiler, stirring constantly until very thick.
5. Remove from heat and add lemon juice.
6. Serve over hot, cooked broccoli.

DILLED TOMATOES

tomatoes (amount depends on how many people you are serving)
dill weed

Slice tomatoes and sprinkle lightly with dill weed. Chill until ready to serve.

CHIFFON CAKE WITH SPICY FRUIT SAUCE

1 cup cake meal, unsifted
1/4 cup potato starch, unsifted
1-1/2 cups sugar
1/2 cup oil
8 eggs, separated
1/2 cup water
1/4 cup lemon juice
1 t grated lemon rind

1. Combine cake meal, potato starch and sugar.
2. Make a well and add in order oil, egg yolks, water, lemon juice and lemon rind. Beat until smooth, about 5 minutes with an electric mixer on medium.
3. Beat egg whites until *very stiff*. Do not underbeat.
4. Pour egg yolk mixture over and gently fold in until blended. Do not stir.
5. Pour into ungreased 10" tube pan and bake at 325° for 1 hour and 10 minutes. Invert immediately and hang over neck of funnel and cool thoroughly.
6. Cut from pan and serve with Spicy Fruit Sauce (recipe follows).

SPICY FRUIT SAUCE

1-1/2 cup dried apricots
1 T lemon juice
1-lb-9-oz jar applesauce
1/4 cup raisins
1 t cinnamon
1/4 t ginger
3 T sugar

1. Place apricots and lemon juice in a saucepan. Add water to cover. Simmer uncovered 30 minutes, until very tender.
2. Beat until mashed or blend in a blender.
3. Add applesauce, raisins, cinnamon, ginger and sugar. Mix well and cook on low for a few more minutes. Serve hot or cold.

LEMON MERINGUE PIE

Crust

1 cup matzo meal
2 T sugar
dash salt
1/4 t cinnamon
1 T sesame seeds
1/2 cup melted pareve margarine

1. Blend all ingredients well. Press into 9" pie pan.
2. Bake at 375° for 15 to 20 minutes. Cool before filling.

Filling

5 T potato starch
1/8 t salt
1 cup sugar
2 cups water
3 eggs, separated (reserve whites for meringue)
2 T pareve margarine
5 T lemon juice
1 T grated lemon rind

1. Combine potato starch, salt, 1/2 cup of the sugar, and the water in the top of a double boiler until thick, stirring constantly. Cover and cook 10 minutes, stirring occasionally.
2. Combine egg yolks and 1/2 cup sugar. Mix in a little of the hot mixture, stirring rapidly until smooth. Pour back into pan. Cook 2 minutes, stirring constantly.
3. Remove from heat. Stir in margarine, lemon juice and lemon rind. Cool to room temperature without stirring. Do not refrigerate.
4. Pour into baked shell. Cover with meringue and seal edges. Bake at 325° for 15 minutes or until light brown. Chill and serve.

Meringue

6 egg whites
6 T sugar

Beat egg whites until foamy. Gradually beat in 6 T sugar until smooth and glossy.

APRIL—EASTER DINNER:

Salad
Cucumber Vinaigrette Salad

Entree
Honey-Glazed Game Hens

Wild Rice Pilaf

Acorn Squash Cups with Peas

Bread
Potato Bread

Dessert
Angel Food Cake

CUCUMBER VINAIGRETTE SALAD

---

2 large cucumbers, thinly sliced

4 4-oz cans pimientos, drained and sliced

2/3 cup vegetable oil

1/4 cup white wine vinegar

1/2 t salt

2 cups sour cream (a maybe)

green onion, for garnish

---

1. Mix together cucumber and pimiento strips.
2. Shake oil, vinegar and salt together.
3. Pour over cucumbers and chill 1 hour. Drain well.
4. Blend in sour cream. Garnish with chopped green onion tops.

HONEY-GLAZED GAME HENS

Recipe found on page 118.

WILD RICE PILAF

1 cup regular white rice (raw)
1 cup wild rice (raw)
1 medium onion, chopped
1 cup celery, chopped
1 cup mushrooms, sliced
2 bay leaves
1/2 t thyme
salt and pepper to taste
1 stick unsalted butter
2 cups chicken bouillon (make your own by boiling a chicken and using the juice or water it was boiled in)

1. Butter sides and bottom of a flat casserole dish.
2. Rinse the rice under cold water and pour into the casserole dish.
3. Sauté the vegetables and seasonings in the stick of butter.
4. Pour out the cooked vegetables over the rice.
5. Pour the prepared bouillon over the rice.
6. Cover the casserole and bake for an hour at 350° or until rice is tender and all the water is absorbed.

ACORN SQUASH CUPS WITH PEAS

Recipe found on page 53.

POTATO BREAD

Recipe found on page 77.

ANGEL FOOD CAKE

Batter

1 cup sifted cake flour
3/4 cup sugar
12 egg white (1-1/2 cups)
1-1/2 t cream of tartar
1-1/2 t imitation vanilla
1/4 t salt
3/4 cup sugar

1. Sift flour and 3/4 cup sugar together. Repeat sifting. Set aside.
2. In a large mixing bowl, beat egg whites with cream of tartar, vanilla and salt at medium speed of electric mixer until soft peaks form.
3. Gradually add remaining 3/4 cup sugar, 2 T at a time. Continue beating until stiff peaks form.
4. Sift about 1/4 of the flour mixture over whites. Fold in.
5. Repeat, folding in remaining flour by fourths.
6. Turn into ungreased 10″ tube pan.
7. Bake in 375° oven 35 to 40 minutes, or until cake tests done.

8. Invert cake in pan on a wire rack. Cool for approximately 10 minutes.
9. Using a spatula, loosen cake from pan. Remove from pan and frost.

Frosting

Either top with fresh fruit and whipped cream or use one of the frosting recipes in the cookbook. Dream Whip is suggested for your diet.

MAY—CINCO DE MAYO, A MEXICAN FIESTA:

Soup
Gazpacho

Salad
Guacamole Salad with Shrimp and Chips

Entree
Tostadas

Spanish Rice

Dessert
Flan

GAZPACHO

---

4 slices bread, torn into pieces

---

4 large ripe tomatoes, chopped (one 20-oz can tomatoes)

---

2 medium cucumbers, chopped

---

1 medium green pepper, chopped

---

1 cup celery, chopped

---

1 medium onion, chopped

---

1 cup water

1/4 cup vegetable oil

1/3 cup tarragon vinegar

---

2 cloves garlic, finely chopped

---

2 t salt

---

1 t ground cumin

1/8 t freshly ground pepper

---

2 cups homemade croutons (recipe in this book)

---

6 celery stalks

---

1. Mix bread, 3/4 of the tomatoes, 1/2 of the cucumber, 1/4 of the green pepper, the celery, 1/2 of the onion, the water and oil in large bowl. Cover and refrigerate 1 hour.
2. Place half the mixture in blender container. Cover and blend on high speed for 8 seconds. Repeat with remaining mixture.
3. Stir in vinegar, garlic, salt, cumin and pepper. Cover and refrigerate at least 2 hours.
4. Place remaining chopped vegetables in small bowls. Cover and refrigerate. Serve as condiments to the soup.
5. Serve the cold soup in chilled dishes with a stalk of celery standing up inside the dish.
6. Garnish with the homemade croutons. This should make 6 servings of about 1/2 cup each.

GUACAMOLE SALAD WITH SHRIMP AND CHIPS

1 cup shrimp, cooked and drained (small or large)
2 medium-size ripe avocados
1 T chopped white onions
1 large tomato, chopped
1/4 cup french dressing (recipe in this book)
1 t finely chopped chilies (optional; omit if you do not care for really hot, spicy food)
1 dash Tabasco sauce
juice of 1/2 lime
salt and pepper to taste
1 head of lettuce, cut into pieces
1/2 cup green peppers, sliced
1 large onion, sliced
2 tomatoes, quartered
taco chips

1. Peel avocados, cut in half and remove pits.
2. Place in a mixing bowl, break up avocado with a fork and stir with wire whisk or mixer until it is smooth but still retains some of its original consistency. Add the onions, chopped tomato, french dressing, chilies, Tabasco, lime juice, salt and pepper. Mix well. Set aside.
3. Place the lettuce in a large bowl. Spoon guacamole over the lettuce, and top with peppers, onions and tomatoes.
4. Place the shrimp on the top and sides of the salad.
5. Serve the salad with taco chips. (The chips are made by frying tortillas until they are hard and crisp. Be careful not to salt them too much.)

TOSTADAS

---

8 six-inch tortillas (available canned, frozen or refrigerated at most grocery stores; recipe for homemade tortillas follows)

---

1 lb ground beef

---

1 large onion, chopped

---

1 clove garlic, chopped

---

1 15-oz can tomato sauce

---

2 t chili powder

---

1 t dried oregano leaves

---

1 t salt

1/4 t dried crushed red peppers

---

refried beans (available canned; recipe for homemade
refried beans follows)

---

4 cups shredded lettuce

---

3 medium tomatoes, sliced

---

1 6-oz jar hot or mild chili salsa

---

8 oz sour cream (a maybe for some people)

---

1. Fry one tortilla at a time until slightly brown and crisp, about 30 seconds
   on each side.
2. Drain on paper towels. Keep warm in oven at a low temperature.
3. Brown beef, onion and garlic until beef is sufficiently done.
4. Stir in tomato sauce, chili powder, oregano, salt and red peppers.
5. Heat to boiling. Reduce heat. Simmer uncovered for 15 minutes.
6. Place 1/4 to 1/3 cup beans on each tortilla. Spread with about 1/3 cup
   meat mixture.
7. Cover each tostada with lettuce. Arrange the tomato slices on top.
8. If your diet permits, top with sour cream and salsa.

TORTILLAS

1/3 cup lard or Crisco
3 cups all-purpose flour
1-1/2 t salt
3/4 cup water

1. Thoroughly cut shortening into flour and salt.
2. Add water. Stir with fork until dough almost cleans side of bowl. Add a little more water if necessary.
3. Turn dough onto lightly floured board. Knead until smooth.
4. Divide into small equal parts, shaping each into a small ball. Roll into circle. Cover with a damp cloth, so that the dough does not dry out.
5. Cook on ungreased hot griddle until brown, turning once.

REFRIED BEANS

2 cups water
8 oz dried pinto beans (about 1-1/4 cups)
1 medium onion, chopped
1 clove garlic, chopped
1 t salt
1 T baking soda
3 T vegetable oil

1. Rinse beans in cold water.
2. Let the beans soak overnight if possible (this softens them and it does not take them as long to cook).
3. Heat the water and add the beans. Begin the boiling process.

4. When the beans begin leaving their skins (about 3-4 hours for unsoaked beans), then add the onion, garlic, salt, baking soda and vegetable oil.
5. Add more hot water to cover the beans.
6. Heat to boiling and reduce heat. Cover and simmer, stirring occasionally, until tender.
7. Stir and mash beans. Add them to your recipe or salt and pepper to taste and eat them as they are.

SPANISH RICE

1/2 stick butter

1/2 cup chopped onions

1 clove garlic, minced

2 T chopped green bell pepper

2 cups long grain rice

1-3/4 cups tomato sauce

3 cups hot chicken stock

1 t salt

1/4 t freshly ground pepper

---

1. In a large skillet, heat half of the butter and sauté the onions, garlic and green pepper until the onions are golden.
2. Heat the rest of the butter in the same pan. Add the rice and cook gently, stirring constantly until the rice is well coated and evenly colored.
3. Add the tomato sauce and heat thoroughly.
4. Add the chicken stock.
5. Cover and cook over low heat for 20 minutes or until the liquid has been absorbed.
6. Season with salt and pepper.

FLAN

Recipe found on page 163.

MAY—MOTHER'S DAY BRUNCH:

Appetizer
Vichyssoise (Cold Potato Soup)

Salad
Sweet Ambrosia

Entree
Chicken Cream Crepes

Dessert
Cold Lemon Soufflé

VICHYSSOISE (COLD POTATO SOUP)

3 cups raw potatoes, diced

2-1/2 cups bouillon or consommé (best if you make your own)

1/3 cup onions, minced

1 t prepared yellow mustard

1-1/2 cups light cream or Coffee Rich or half and half

1/2 t salt

1/8 t pepper

small bunch parsley

1. Cover diced potatoes with bouillon in saucepan. Boil 10 minutes.
2. Add onions and continue cooking until potatoes are tender.
3. Put mixture through a ricer or sieve. Stir in mustard.
4. Add cream, salt and pepper.
5. Cool. Then chill thoroughly. Serve in chilled soup cups.
6. Garnish with a sprig of parsley. Yields 4-6 servings.

SWEET AMBROSIA

1-1/2 cups of the following fruits and their juices:

watermelon balls when in season

honeydew melon balls when in season

cantaloupe balls

orange sections (mandarin)

papayas

peaches

strawberries

cherries

fruit cocktail (in most cases this is good except for the pineapple)

1-1/2 cups freshly squeezed orange juice. Canned is fine if fresh is not available.

1-1/2 cups bananas to be added just before serving. This is to prevent them from browning.

1 medium chunk of crystallized ginger root chopped up in noticeable pieces so it can easily be removed before serving

1 medium-size lemon

---

1. Scoop out the watermelon balls from the watermelon.
2. Save 1/2 of the watermelon so you can use this to marinate and eventually serve the fruit in.
3. After all the fruit has been prepared, mix together in the melon half and pour the orange juice over. Remember to save the bananas until you are ready to serve.
4. Mix in the chunks of ginger and squeeze the lemon over all.
5. Usually ambrosia is served with coconut flakes, but this is an absolute no-no for migraine patients!
6. Remember to remove the ginger pieces. If and when they are tasted, they are very bitter.

7. This is particularly good when prepared hours ahead of time or even the night before.
8. An easy, good, warm weather treat. It also lasts in the refrigerator a week or so—but usually it is consumed quickly.
9. This serves a large crowd.

CHICKEN CREAM CREPES

---

4 chicken breasts, cooked in 6 cups boiling water. Save this liquid after boiling and use it for your potato soup bouillon. Also save 2 cups of this broth for the sauce.

Sauce

---

6 T flour

---

1 cube (1/2 cup) butter

---

2 cups milk

---

2 cups chicken broth

---

salt and pepper

1/2 cup onion, chopped

---

1 can dehydrated vegetables (flakes)

1/2 cup chopped mushrooms

---

1. Combine the flour and butter.
2. Gradually add the milk and then add the chicken broth to the flour mixture.
3. Mix sauce until thick—keep tasting.
4. Add salt and pepper to taste, then add onion and dry vegetables.
5. Continue to stir mixture over low heat.
6. Add chicken, cut into bite-size pieces.
7. Sauté the mushrooms in butter for a very short while.
8. Garnish the sauce-covered crepes with the mushrooms.

BASIC CREPE RECIPE

1 cup all-purpose flour
1-1/2 cups milk
2 eggs
1 T cooking oil
1/4 t salt
1 t sugar

1. In a mixing bowl, combine flour, milk, eggs, oil, salt and sugar. Mix until blended very smooth.
2. Heat a lightly greased 6-inch skillet or an inverted crepe pan. (I spray my crepe pan with a vegetable cooking spray, Pam.) If you choose to use the electric inverted-type skillet, cook the crepes according to the manufacturer's directions.
3. Pour the batter into a shallow bowl or pie plate. If using the inverted crepe pan, dip the heated pan, rounded side down, into the batter. Hold for a few seconds to be sure the surface is completely covered. Quickly turn right side up. Do not give up if you lose the first couple. If the batter does not stay on the pan it is because the pan is too hot or there is too much oil or spray on the pan.
4. After the skillet has been covered with the batter, return it to the range top and continue to cook the crepe for about 45 seconds or until it has turned a light brown. (You do not brown the crepe on the second side. The unbrowned side is the side that is filled.)
5. Hold the browned crepe over a paper towel and loosen the crepe with a spatula.
6. You may stack the crepes after each crepe has completely cooled. Use two layers of waxed paper in between them. This recipe should make about 16 successful crepes. If you wish to make a double batch and store some, it is good to know that the crepes freeze well as long as they have the waxed paper between them and are then stored in a vaporproof bag. You may freeze them for no longer than four months.

COLD LEMON SOUFFLÉ

---

5 eggs

1-1/2 cups sugar

juice (3/4 cup) and grated rind of 3 large lemons

2 pkg gelatin (unflavored)

1/2 cup water

1 t sugar

2 cups Dream Whip, partially whipped. Remember, *no* real cream!

pinch of salt

1/8 t cream of tartar

1/4 cup macadamia nuts, crushed (these are a maybe)

3/4 cup heavy cream, whipped (a maybe)

2 T ground macadamia nuts

---

1. Butter and sugar a 1-1/2 qt soufflé dish. Tie a collar of oiled and sugared wax paper or aluminum foil around the mold to extend the sides. (Be sure to use oil on the collar. Butter will solidify when chilled and the soufflé will stick to the paper.)
2. Separate the eggs and beat the yolks with the sugar and lemon rind, adding the lemon juice gradually until the mixture is very thick and mousse-like. Do not underbeat.
3. Sprinkle the gelatin over the water to soften. Add 1 t sugar and stir over low heat to dissolve the gelatin. Cool and add to the lemon mixture, combining thoroughly.
4. Fold in the partially whipped Dream Whip.
5. Beat the egg whites with the salt and cream of tartar until stiff peaks form.
6. Fold into the lemon mixture.
7. Turn into the prepared soufflé dish and chill in the refrigerator until set.

8. Remove the collar and decorate the sides of the soufflé with macadamia nut crumbs and the top with the whipped cream and nut crumbs. Mom will love her special treat.

JUNE—ENJOYING THE CULINARY ART OF GREECE:

Appetizer
Stuffed Grape Leaves

Soup
Lemon Egg Soup

Salad
A La "Grecque" Salad with Spinach Yogurt Dressing

Entree
Moussaka

Meatballs with Avgolemona Sauce

Dessert
Baklava

LEMON EGG SOUP

1 qt chicken broth
1/2 cup washed rice
3 eggs
juice of 2 lemons

1. Bring chicken broth to a boil. Add rice and cook until tender.
2. Beat eggs until light and frothy. Then slowly beat in lemon juice.
3. Add a little of the hot broth to the egg mixture, blending it in well. Slowly add egg to broth, stirring constantly.
4. Heat through but do not boil.
5. Garnish with thin slices of lemon. Serves 6.

A LA "GRECQUE" SALAD

1 10-oz pkg frozen cauliflower clusters
1 10-oz pkg frozen broccoli florets
1 10-oz pkg frozen carrot slices
1-1/4 cups chicken broth
1 cup cherry tomatoes
1/3 cup vegetable broth, reserved from cooking vegetables
1/3 cup vinegar
2 T vegetable oil
1 bay leaf
1 clove garlic, sliced

1. Place the frozen vegetables in a large skillet with the chicken broth. Cover and cook for 4 minutes. (If using fresh vegetables, cook till just tender.) Remove from skillet and drain, reserving 1/3 cup of vegetable broth. Add the cherry tomatoes to the cooked vegetables.
2. Combine the reserved vegetable broth with the oil, vinegar, bay leaf and garlic; pour over the vegetables. Cover and refrigerate for at least 1 hour.
3. When ready to serve, drain the vegetables and reserve the marinade. Arrange the vegetables on a platter and serve with Spinach Yogurt Dressing. (Recipe follows.)

SPINACH YOGURT DRESSING

1 10-oz pkg frozen chopped spinach, thawed and drained
2 8-oz containers plain yogurt
1/2 t dill weed
reserved marinade (from A La Grecque Salad), with bay leaf and garlic removed

Combine all of the ingredients in a blender jar, and blend until smooth, approximately 2 minutes. Serve on the side with your vegetable platter.

MOUSSAKA

1 large eggplant or 2 medium (about 2 lb)
4 T unsalted butter
3/4 lb ground round beef
3/4 lb ground lamb (if possible, have beef and lamb ground together)
2 medium onions, chopped
1 clove garlic, whole
1 15-oz can tomato sauce
3/4 cup beef broth
1 T snipped parsley
1 t salt
1/4 t pepper
1/4 t ground nutmeg
2/3 cup dry bread crumbs
2 eggs, beaten
flour
tomato sauce (recipe follows)
white sauce (recipe follows)

1. Cut unpared eggplant crosswise into 1/2-inch slices.
2. Sprinkle eggplant slices with a little salt and place on a paper towel. Let them sit for about 15 minutes. (The salt will help remove some of the moisture from the eggplant.)
3. While you are waiting for the eggplant slices to drain, you may prepare the meat mixture.
4. In a large skillet, sauté onions and garlic in butter until transparent.
5. Cook lamb and beef with the onions and garlic until the meat is slightly browned. Drain.
6. Stir in the tomato sauce, beef broth, parsley, salt, pepper and nutmeg. Cook uncovered over medium heat until half the liquid is absorbed, about 20 to 30 minutes. Now go back to the eggplant slices.

7. After the slices have had a chance to drain, run them under a little cold water to rinse off the salt and blot with a paper towel.
8. In a frying pan, melt 2 T butter. Dust slices of eggplant with a little flour and dip in the beaten egg. Brown a few slices at a time in hot butter.
9. Line your casserole dish or cake pan with a layer of the slices. Now prepare the white sauce.

WHITE SAUCE FOR MOUSSAKA

1/4 cup butter
1/4 cup all-purpose flour
3/4 t salt
1/4 t ground nutmeg
2 cups milk
2 eggs, slightly beaten

1. Heat butter until melted.
2. Blend in flour, salt and nutmeg. Cook over low heat, stirring constantly until smooth and bubbly. Remove from heat.
3. Stir in milk. Heat to boiling, stirring constantly.
4. Boil and stir constantly for 1 minute.
5. Gradually stir at least 1/4 of the hot milk mixture into the eggs. Now beat back into sauce and add to the rest of the mixture.
6. Now go back to the moussaka meat mixture. Return to the stove and heat. Stir 2/3 cup bread crumbs and the eggs into meat mixture. Cover the layer of eggplant which you have set aside in the casserole dish with a layer of the meat mixture. Alternate layers with eggplant slices and meat.
7. Now pour the white sauce over the mixture.
8. Cook uncovered in 375° oven for 45 minutes.
9. Prepare tomato sauce. Let moussaka stand 20 minutes before serving. Cut into squares. Serve with tomato sauce.

TOMATO SAUCE FOR MOUSSAKA

1 medium onion, finely chopped
1 clove garlic, finely chopped
1 T vegetable oil
2 cups ripe tomatoes, chopped
1/2 cup water
1-1/2 t salt
1 t dried basil leaves
1/2 t sugar
1/4 t pepper
1 bay leaf, crushed
1 6-oz can tomato paste

1. Cook and stir onion and garlic in oil until onion is tender.
2. Add remaining ingredients except tomato paste. Heat to boiling, stirring constantly. Reduce heat. Let thicken for about 30 minutes, then stir in the tomato paste. You may want to add a little water to get the desired consistency.
3. Serve this alongside the moussaka.

STUFFED GRAPE LEAVES

4 cups finely chopped onions
3/4 cup olive or cooking oil
1 cup silver pearl rice
1/4 cup water
1/8 cup dill weed
juice of 1 lemon
pepper to taste
50 grape leaves, canned or fresh

1. Sauté onions in oil.
2. Mix well with remaining ingredients (except grape leaves) and cook over low heat, stirring to prevent sticking.
3. Cool. May be cooked the day before and refrigerated.
4. Wash about 50 canned or fresh grape leaves. (Preservative may contain salt.)
5. Squeeze out excess water and cut off stems. Spread leaf on plate, vein side up with the stem end facing you.
6. Place approximately 1 t of filling on the end nearest you, fold over sides and roll away from you, keeping sides tucked in.
7. Cover bottom of pan with a few extra leaves. Then place rolled leaves in pan, seam side down, until layer is completed. Repeat until all the leaves are used up.
8. Pour mixture of 1-3/4 cup water and 1 t olive or cooking oil over finished rolls.
9. Place ovenproof plate over rolls. Cover and cook in a 325°–350° oven for 1-1/2 hours.
10. Cool before removing plate to prevent discoloring. Serve cold, garnished with lemon slices.

MEATBALLS WITH AVGOLEMONA SAUCE

(The National Sauce of Greece)

Meatballs

3/4 lb of ground round beef
3/4 lb ground lamb
1 medium onion, finely chopped
1/2 cup rice, uncooked
salt and pepper
1 egg, beaten
parsley, chopped very fine or dried (preferably dried)
2 T butter
beef broth, boiling

1. Mix together meat, onion, rice and seasoning. Bind with egg.
2. Form into small balls the size of walnuts and roll in parsley.
3. Melt butter in pan, lower heat and place meatballs in rows. Pour in enough boiling beef broth to cover completely. Simmer over low heat for about 30 minutes.
4. Serve over regular white rice.

Avgolemona Sauce

6 egg yolks
2 whole eggs
8 T lemon juice
hot beef broth

1. Beat yolks and eggs until thick and lemon-colored. Slowly stir in lemon juice.
2. Remove some of the hot broth from the meatballs and add slowly to egg-lemon mixture. Pour sauce over meatballs and cook over low heat until it comes to a boil.

BAKLAVA

1-1/2 cups honey
1/2 cup water
1 T lemon juice
1 t vanilla
1 pkg filo pastry dough or pastry leaves (available in frozen food sections of grocery or specialty stores)
1-1/2 pounds unsalted butter, clarified
3 cups finely chopped unsalted macadamia nuts
2 T cinnamon
1 T allspice
whole cloves

1. Boil the honey, water, lemon juice and vanilla in a saucepan until it has the consistency of a thick syrup, about 10 minutes. Set aside to cool.
2. Cut the filo (pastry sheets) to fit a cake pan. The filo dries out quickly after opening—you may have to wrap it in a slightly damp cloth.
3. Mix together the nuts, cinnamon, and allspice. Set aside.
4. Brush your cake pan with melted butter. Layer 6 sheets of pastry in the bottom of the pan, brushing each lightly with the melted butter and the nut-spice mixture. Use scraps of pastry too, especially in the middle where it really doesn't make a difference. Save the good sheets for the last six, if you can. This holds the pieces together, and is also the section that is noticed.
5. When the pan is full, add these 6 or more final sheets with no nuts, just butter. Do not use the sediment in the bottom of the butter.
6. With a sharp knife, cut the baklava into 1-1/2″ pieces. Cut diagonally to form diamonds. Stick a clove in the center of each slice. Heat any remaining butter (not sediment) and pour into the knife slits.
7. Bake at 300° for 1 to 1-1/4 hours, until lightly browned and rather dry-looking.
8. Pour the cooled syrup (made in step #1) over the cooked baklava slowly, continuing to pour until no more is absorbed. This may be served immediately, but gets even better upon standing.

JULY—INDEPENDENCE DAY PICNIC GOODIES:

Appetizers
Fresh Vegetable Tray with Corky's Dill Dip

Salad
Macaroni Salad

Jello/Fruit Mold

Entree
Chicken Bar-B-Que

Scalloped Potatoes

Dessert
Oatmeal Cookies

Lemon Bars

Watermelon

Beverage
Apple Punch Delight—A Southern Treat

FRESH VEGETABLE TRAY

Your choice of fresh vegetables, such as broccoli buds, asparagus, carrot sticks, zucchini slices, cucumber slices, whole mushrooms, green onions, and green peppers

1. Blanch the broccoli, asparagus and cauliflower in a little garlic and salt water to tenderize them.
2. Place your vegetables on a platter or in individual bowls.
3. After preparing the vegetables for your special day, be sure to keep them in a crisper in the refrigerator.
4. Serve with the following dip.

CORKY'S DILL DIP

2/3 cup sour cream
2/3 cup Miracle Whip salad dressing
1 T parsley flakes
1 T dill weed
1 T garlic salt
1 T rosemary
1 T chopped green onion
1 T tarragon
1 chopped hard-boiled egg
pinch of freshly ground pepper

Mix together all ingredients and store in refrigerator until ready to use. Dip improves upon standing and can be made the day before.

MACARONI SALAD

1/2 7-oz pkg (1 cup) shell macaroni
1 cup chopped celery
1/4 medium onion, chopped
1/4 cup chopped green pepper
1/4 cup chopped pimiento (optional)
1 cup small fresh shrimp (cleaned and cooked) or 1 7-oz can, drained
2 hard-boiled eggs, chopped
1/4 t salt
1/4 t paprika
1 cup Miracle Whip salad dressing
1/4 cup french dressing

1. Cook macaroni. Drain and chill.
2. Add celery, onion, green pepper, pimiento, shrimp, eggs and seasonings.
3. Moisten with the Miracle Whip and the french dressing.
4. Garnish with hard-cooked eggs or tomato slices.
5. Remember to keep this refrigerated. Salad dressing can cause the food to spoil quickly.

JELLO/FRUIT MOLD

1-1/2 cups water
1 envelope gelatin
3/4 cup sugar
1 cup sour cream
1-1/2 t vanilla

1. Heat the water, gelatin and sugar until jello and sugar are dissolved.
2. In another bowl, mix the sour cream and vanilla. Add to the jello mixture slowly.
3. Set in refrigerator to thicken, at least 2 hours.
4. After the jello has set, fold in your fresh fruit. Any fruit will do. We particularly like peaches and berries.
5. Top with Dream Whip.

CHICKEN BAR-B-QUE (SPICY)

1/4 cup finely chopped onion
1 clove garlic, minced
2 T vegetable oil
3/4 cup catsup
1/3 cup vinegar
1 t grated lemon peel
1 T lemon juice
1 T Worcestershire sauce (this is a maybe: beware)
2 t sugar
1 t dry mustard
1/4 t pepper
1/4 t bottled hot pepper sauce
2 2-1/2-to-3-lb ready-to-cook broiler-fryer chickens

1. Cook onion and garlic in oil until tender but not brown.
2. Stir in catsup, vinegar, lemon peel and juice, Worcestershire sauce (a maybe), sugar, dry mustard, pepper and bottled hot pepper sauce.
3. Simmer, covered, for about 25 to 30 minutes. Stir occasionally.
4. Quarter chickens. Break wing, hip and drumstick joints of chickens so pieces will remain flat. Twist wing tips under back. Season chicken pieces with additional pepper.
5. Place chicken pieces, bone side down, over medium hot coals. Grill chicken about 25 minutes.
6. Brush chicken with sauce every 10 minutes. Makes 8 servings.

SCALLOPED POTATOES
THE EASY WAY

2-lb bag frozen hash browns

1 10-1/2-oz can cream of mushroom soup

1 10-1/2-oz can cream of celery soup

1 8-oz container cultured sour cream

1/2 cup onion flakes (may increase or decrease to taste)

salt and pepper to taste

butter

parsley flakes (for garnish)

---

1. Combine the above and place in a greased cake pan.
2. Sprinkle with parsley flakes and dot with butter.
3. Bake in 350° oven for 1-1/2 to 2 hours.

OATMEAL COOKIES

---

1 cup soft shortening or butter

1-1/2 cups brown sugar, packed

2 eggs

1-3/4 cups flour

3/4 t baking soda

1 t salt

1/2 t cinnamon

1/2 t powdered cloves

1/4 cup sour milk (Add 1 t vinegar to 1/4 cup milk. Let set for 10 minutes.)

1-1/2 cups uncooked oats

1 cup raisins

---

1. Mix the shortening, brown sugar and eggs.
2. In a separate bowl, sift the flour, baking soda, salt, cinnamon and cloves.
3. Combine the shortening mixture with the flour mixture. Add the sour milk, oats and raisins.
4. Drop by rounded teaspoonfuls onto a greased cookie sheet. Bake at 375° for 10 to 15 minutes, or until cookies are brown and are loose on cookie sheet.

LEMON BARS

Recipe found on page 187.

APPLE PUNCH DELIGHT
A SOUTHERN TREAT

6 regular-size tea bags
3 cups boiling water
1 qt apple juice
2 T lemon juice
sugar to taste
1 fresh lemon (for garnish)

1. Place tea bags in a teapot. Pour freshly boiling water over tea bags.
2. Brew 5 minutes. Pour into a larger pitcher.
3. Stir in apple juice and lemon juice.
4. Sweeten to taste with sugar.
5. Pour over ice cubes in tall glasses. Garnish each with a lemon wedge, if you wish. Makes 8 servings.

AUGUST—ITALIAN CUISINE:

Appetizer
Antipasto

Soup
Tomato-Garlic Vegetable Soup

Entree
Pork Chops Italiano

Pasta Side Dish

Fresh Asparagus Sauté

Dessert
Strawberry Water Ice

Crostata

TOMATO-GARLIC VEGETABLE SOUP

8 cups chicken broth, preferably homemade

3 medium potatoes, peeled and cubed

3 medium carrots, sliced very thin

2 stalks celery, sliced thin

1 medium onion, chopped

1 9-oz pkg frozen cut green beans (This is a maybe on our food list.)

pepper to taste

1 cup sliced zucchini

1/2 cup barley

1 6-oz can tomato paste

1/3 cup snipped parsley

2 t dried basil, crushed

1/4 to 1/2 t garlic powder

1 T vegetable oil

1. In a large kettle or dutch oven, prepare your chicken broth. (The reason it is important in our recipes to make your own broth is because prepared ones are usually too salty and salt is a no-no on your diet. To prepare your broth, take a whole chicken and cook it in 9 cups of water until the chicken is tender. Take the chicken out; you may add it to another recipe.

2. In a large kettle or dutch oven, combine your chicken broth, potatoes, carrots, celery, onion, green beans and pepper. Bring this to a boil. Reduce heat, cover and simmer for 10 minutes. Add the zucchini and barley and simmmer for 10 to 15 minutes longer, until the vegetables are very tender.

3. In a little bowl, combine the tomato paste, the spices, and the vegetable oil. Stir this into the soup and continue to simmer until you are ready to serve it. It is a very quick recipe except for making the bouillon, but that is really not difficult. This makes 10 to 12 one-cup servings.

ANTIPASTO

chopped lettuce
artichokes
cauliflower
celery
carrots
cucumbers
onions
mushrooms (optional)
sweet and hot peppers (optional)
cervelat salami, very thinly sliced (This is a maybe on our food list.)
1 cup vegetable oil
1/2 cup tarragon vinegar
1/4 cup sliced green onion
2 T snipped parsley
1 T sugar
1 T lemon juice
2 cloves garlic, minced
1 t salt
1 t dried thyme, crushed
1/8 t cayenne

1. To prepare the artichokes, trim the stem and remove the loose outer leaves from each fresh artichoke. Cut 1 inch off the top. Snip off the leaf tips. Cut each artichoke lengthwise into 6 wedges. Remove or discard the fuzzy or choke part. Brush cut edges with lemon juice. In a large covered kettle, cook in boiling water for 20 to 30 minutes, until they are tender. It is also possible to cook frozen artichokes according to package directions, and that would do just as well and would be a lot quicker.

2. To prepare the fresh cauliflower, just remove the leaves and the woody stem from a head. Then break the head into flowerets and cook in a small amount of boiling water for 10 minutes, or just until tender. You can substitute frozen cauliflower, but fresh is better.
3. Clean the carrots, celery, cucumbers and onions, and cut into bite-size pieces (not too small). The celery, carrots and cucumbers can be sliced or cut into small chunks, and the onions can be cut into rings, quarters or eighths, depending on size.
4. To make the marinade, combine the oil, vinegar, green onion, parsley, sugar, lemon juice, garlic, salt, thyme and cayenne in a screw-top jar. Cover and shake well.
5. Pour the marinade over the vegetables and mix thoroughly. Refrigerate for several hours or overnight, stirring occasionally. If using the mushrooms, slice them and add them to the marinade one hour before you plan to serve the antipasto.
6. When ready to serve, drain the vegetables and arrange them with the salami and peppers (if using) on a platter lined with chopped lettuce.

PORK CHOPS ITALIANO

6 loin pork chops, 1 inch thick
1/2 cup white wine
1/2 t oregano
1/4 t thyme
1 whole clove garlic (optional)
1 bay leaf
1 8-oz can tomato sauce
1 T cooking oil
1 green pepper, finely sliced
1/2 lb mushrooms, thinly sliced

1. Brown pork chops on both sides over medium heat. Remove chops.
2. Add wine, oregano, thyme, garlic and bay leaf, and simmer for 10 minutes. Stir in tomato sauce, add pork chops, and baste with sauce. Cover and simmer for 45 to 50 minutes, basting occasionally.
3. Meanwhile, heat oil in a small, heavy frying pan. Add peppers and mushrooms, and sauté for 3 to 4 minutes.
4. Add sautéed vegetables to chops. Cover and simmer for 10 more minutes. Serves 6.

PASTA SIDE DISH

Tomato Sauce

1 T butter or margarine
2 lb (approximately 6 medium) fresh tomatoes, cut up, or 1 28-oz can of tomatoes, finely chopped
1/2 t salt
1/8 t pepper
1/2 cup snipped parsley
1 or 2 garlic cloves, minced
1/4 cup chopped onion
1 T fresh basil or 1/2 t dried basil, crushed
1 small can tomato paste
1 t sugar

1. If you are using fresh tomatoes, bring the tomatoes to a boil in an uncovered saucepan, and cook for about 45 minutes, until they are very tender. Pass the tomatoes through a food mill or sieve, and then discard the skins and seeds. (As you can probably tell, it is easier to use canned tomatoes. Heat in a medium-size saucepan.)
2. Add the spices to the warm tomatoes and cook for about 45 minutes. Then add the sugar and the tomato paste to this, and add it to the pasta of your choice. Heat through before serving.

FRESH ASPARAGUS SAUTÉ

1 lb fresh asparagus, sliced into 1/2″ pieces on the bias
1/2 cup chopped onions
1/2 cup chopped celery
2 T margarine
1/8 t ground nutmeg
salt and pepper to taste

1. In a covered saucepan, cook the asparagus in a small amount of boiling water for just a couple of minutes, until it turns a bright, pretty green color. Then drain it.
2. In a large frying pan, melt butter and sauté onions and celery in this, adding your nutmeg. Then add salt and pepper to taste and add asparagus, turning occasionally, just to heat through and completely coat the asparagus with butter. Keep this warm and ready to serve next to the pasta.

STRAWBERRY WATER ICE

2 cups sugar
1 cup water
4 pt fresh, ripe strawberries, washed and hulled
1/3 cup orange juice
1/4 cup lemon juice

1. Stir sugar and water together in a saucepan, and bring to a boil over medium heat. Boil and stir for 5 minutes. Remove and let cool.
2. Puree the strawberries in an electric blender or food mill. Add orange juice and lemon juice. Combine with cooled syrup. Mix well.
3. Pour into low, flat pans or refrigerator trays, cover tightly and freeze.
4. Remove from freezer to refrigerator about 45 minutes before serving time to allow to soften slightly. Spoon into sherbet dishes. Top each dish with a whole strawberry and serve with your favorite vanilla wafer. Makes 2 qt water ice. Raspberries may be substituted for strawberries if you prefer a change.

CROSTATA

3 cups all-purpose flour
1/2 cup sugar
1 T baking powder
dash salt
1 cup margarine
2 slightly beaten eggs
1/4 cup milk
1 t imitation almond extract
2 T milk, again
1 10-oz jar cherry preserves

1. In a large mixing bowl, stir together flour, sugar, baking powder and salt. Cut in the margarine until the mixture is kind of crumbly. Then mix 2 eggs, 1/4 cup milk and extract. Add to the dry ingredients and mix well. Turn this out onto a floured surface and knead until it is smooth, about 2 minutes.
2. Set aside 1/3 of the dough. Then blend 2 T milk into the remaining dough and kind of pat it down into a 15 by 10 by 1 inch baking pan.
3. Pour the preserves into a bowl, stirring them enough to get them to one consistency or to break up the large pieces of fruit. Spoon these preserves over the dough which you have already patted into the pan.
4. Roll the reserved dough into a 12 by 10 inch rectangle. Cut crosswise into 1/2-inch-wide strips. Lay the strips an inch apart across the dough and then arrange the remaining strips atop, getting a diamond-shaped pattern.
5. Bake this in a 400° oven for 18 to 20 minutes, and then cut into bars. It makes approximately 40, depending on the size of the pieces.

SEPTEMBER—MOTHER'S BACK-TO-SCHOOL LUNCH:

Soup
Chilled Tomato Soup

Entree
Crepes

Salad
Chinese Salad

Dessert
Date-Filled Sugar Cookies

CHILLED TOMATO SOUP

1 10-3/4 oz can condensed tomato soup
1-3/4 cup milk
1 8-oz carton plain yogurt (a maybe)
2 T vegetable oil
2 T tarragon vinegar
1 clove garlic, finely chopped (a maybe)
1/4 t celery salt
1/2 t onion powder

1. In a bowl, blend tomato soup, milk, yogurt, oil, vinegar, garlic and spices. Cover this and chill thoroughly.
2. When you are ready to serve, add a little dab of yogurt on top.

CREPES

Crepes are great microwave "warmups."

1 cup all-purpose flour
1-1/2 cups milk
2 eggs
1 T vegetable oil
1/4 t salt

1. Combine flour, milk, eggs, oil and salt in a bowl until blended.
2. There are two basic kinds of crepe pans. There is the electric one which is terrific because it has exact temperature settings, and then there is the conventional one which is a 6-inch skillet (you have to heat this and then, when it gets hot, start adding batter to it). I am going to assume that you know how to use a crepe pan. (You may refer to page 281, the Basic Crepe Recipe, for an outlined procedure on making crepes.) Of course, to start this off, you have to grease the pan a little bit. Remove it from heat and spoon about 2 T of batter into it. Lift and tilt the skillet evenly and then return to heat. Brown the crepe on one side only. (You also may be cooking on an inverted crepe pan, which is better than a skillet.) In order to remove the crepe, invert the pan over a paper towel. Repeat with the remaining batter. This recipe will make approximately 18 crepes and you have to continually grease the skillet while coking. Actually, you will have to experiment with this to get it exactly the way you like it.

Sauce and Filling

---

6 T margarine

---

6 T all-purpose flour

---

dash salt

---

3 cups milk

1/4 cup dry white wine*

---

1 2-1/2 oz jar sliced, drained mushrooms or 1 cup fresh
  mushrooms, sliced

---

1 10-oz pkg chopped broccoli

---

2 cups finely chopped, cooked chicken

1/2 cup finely chopped or crumbled french bread

---

*Wine on its own is an absolute no-no; however, when cooked, the alcohol
which causes the problems for migraine patients is cooked out of it and
what we really get is the taste. If you are still afraid of using it, you may
delete it. It is an experimental ingredient.

Sauce

1. In a medium saucepan, melt the margarine.
2. Blend in the flour and salt.
3. Add the milk all at once.
4. Cook this, stirring constantly until thick and bubbly.
5. Stir in the crumbled french bread and wine until warmed through.
   Remove 1/2 cup of sauce and set aside. Stir the mushrooms into the
   remaining sauce.

Filling

1. Cook the broccoli according to package directions. Drain.
2. Combine drained broccoli and chicken with the 1/2 cup of reserved
   sauce.

Assembly

1. Spread 1/4 cup filling over the unbrowned side of the crepe. Leave 1/2-inch rim around the edge and then roll up crepe.
2. Place seam side of the crepe down in the skillet and then repeat this until you are finished with your crepes.
3. Drizzle sauce over the crepes and then cook, covered, on low heat until bubbly. You may place crepes and sauce in a chafing dish or baking dish. Place in your oven for 1/2 hour. Bake this at just 250° to keep it warm. All of the ingredients are completely cooked.

CHINESE SALAD

1 small can chow mein noodles

1 head lettuce

3 green onions, chopped

1 small cucumber, chopped

1 T toasted sesame seeds (a maybe)

1 small can drained mandarin oranges

1 cup green grapes, cut in halves

Dressing

5 T sugar

7 T rice vinegar

1/2 t salt

1 t pepper

1 t lemon juice

1/4 t five spice powder (a premixed combination of spices often used in Chinese cooking)

1/4 cup vegetable oil

1. Mix the salad ingredients together and toss just before serving.
2. Mix the dressing ingredients together. Pour over the salad and toss.

DATE-FILLED SUGAR COOKIES

2 cups snipped pitted dates
1/2 cup water
1/3 cup granulated sugar
2 T lemon juice
1/4 t salt
1 cup vegetable shortening
1/2 cup granulated sugar
1/2 cup packed brown sugar
1 egg
3 T milk
1 t vanilla
3 cups all-purpose flour
1/2 t baking soda
1/2 t salt

1. In a saucepan, combine dates, water and 1/3 cup granulated sugar. Bring to a boil. Cover and simmer for about 5 minutes, stirring often. Add lemon juice and 1/4 t salt to this; cool and set aside.
2. In another bowl, cream shortening and the next two ingredients. Add eggs, milk and vanilla, and beat well. Stir together flour, baking soda and 1/2 t salt. Add to the creamed mixture and mix well. Cover and chill for 1 hour in refrigerator.
3. Divide the dough in half. On a floured surface, roll each portion to 1/8" thickness. Cut into 2-1/2-inch rounds with a cookie cutter.

4. Top half of the rounds with a scant tablespoon of the cooled date mixture and then, with a tiny cutter or thimble, cut a small hole in the center of the remaining rounds. (If you prefer a covered cookie, leave the top round of dough whole.) Place on the date-topped round and seal the edge of the cookie with an inverted teaspoon tip or fork. Place 1 inch apart on an ungreased cookie sheet. Bake at 350° for 10 to 12 minutes. This makes approximately 30 cookies. (I have also doubled this recipe and it has worked quite well.)

OCTOBER—OCTOBER FEST:

Soup
Cream of Mushroom Soup

Salad
Three Bean Salad

German Potato Salad

Entree
Crock Pot Sauerbraten

Cabbage with Onion and Apple

Bread
Pumpernickel Rye Bread

Dessert
Apple Streusel

Pumpkin Cookies

CREAM OF MUSHROOM SOUP

1 lb fresh mushrooms, sliced
2 cups half and half (a maybe on some people's diets)
4 cups chicken stock, preferably your own
1/2 cup green onion, chopped
1/4 cup butter
1 T flour
white pepper to taste
salt to taste (salt is a maybe)

1. After you have sliced the mushrooms and prepared your own chicken stock, sauté the chopped onion in the butter. Add the flour and mix continually until the mixture is the consistency of a pasty roux.
2. Warm the half and half in a skillet or saucepan on low heat, being careful not to boil or scorch it. Add the onion-flour mixture, then add the sliced mushrooms. Gradually mix in the chicken stock, stirring constantly to maintain a smooth consistency. Add salt (optional) and pepper to taste. This is really quite an easy recipe, as long as you remember to cook all of the ingredients over low heat so that they do not boil or scorch.

THREE BEAN SALAD

---

1 16-oz can (equalling 2 cups) green beans, drained

1 16-oz can (or 2 cups) cut yellow wax beans, drained (This is a maybe.)

1 16-oz can red kidney beans, drained

1 medium green pepper, sliced

1 medium onion, thinly sliced

Dressing

1/2 cup sugar

1/2 cup white vinegar

1/2 cup salad oil

1 t salt (maybe)

1/2 t tarragon

1/2 t basil

2 T parsley

1 very small jar pimientos

1/4 cup sunflower seeds (This is a maybe.)

---

1. Combine the dressing ingredients, mixing them well.
2. Drizzle this over the vegetables.
3. Cover and marinate several hours or overnight. Stir the beans several times while you are marinating them. When you are ready to serve, drain the dressing off the vegetables.

GERMAN POTATO SALAD

6 medium potatoes (2 lb)
6 slices cervelat salami (This is a maybe.)
1/2 cup chopped onion
2 T all-purpose flour
2 T sugar
1/2 t salt (This is a maybe.)
1 t celery seed
dash pepper
1 cup water
1/2 cup white vinegar
2 hard-boiled eggs, sliced

1. In a covered saucepan, cook the potatoes in boiling water for 25 to 30 minutes or until tender. Drain them. Peel and slice the potatoes.
2. Cut the cervelat salami into small pieces. In a large skillet, cook the salami until it is fairly crisp. Drain this, reserving 1/4 cup drippings. Set the salami aside.
3. Cook the onion in the reserved drippings until it is tender but not brown.
4. Blend the flour, sugar, salt, celery seed and pepper. Add water and vinegar. Cook and stir until thick.
5. Add the salami bits and potatoes. Cook about 5 minutes or until heated through, tossing lightly.
6. Add hard-boiled eggs and toss slightly, just to mix with the vegetables. Serve this warm. Makes 6 to 8 servings.

CROCK POT SAUERBRATEN

3-1/2 to 4 lbs beef rump or sirloin tip

1 cup water

1 cup mild vinegar

1 large onion, sliced

1 lemon, sliced

10 whole cloves

4 bay leaves, broken in half

6 whole peppercorns

2 T sugar

1 clove garlic, sliced (optional)

12 gingersnaps, crushed

---

1. Place meat in a deep ceramic or glass bowl. Combine water, vinegar, onion, lemon, cloves, bay leaves, peppercorns, sugar and garlic, and pour over meat. Cover and refrigerate for 24 to 36 hours. Do not marinate for longer than 36 hours or the meat will be too sour. Turn meat several times while marinating.
2. Place meat in crock pot, pour 1 cup marinade over meat, cover and cook on low for 6 to 8 hours. Remove to warm platter. Strain meat juices, return juices to crock pot and add gingersnaps. Cook on high for 10 to 15 minutes. Pour over meat and serve. Makes 8 servings.

CABBAGE WITH ONION AND APPLE

1 medium head of green cabbage, cored and thinly sliced
4 T butter or margarine
1 small onion, thinly sliced
1 tart apple, finely chopped or grated
1/4 cup dry white wine (wine is okay here because it gets cooked)
1 T brown sugar

1. Melt butter or margarine in heavy skillet and sauté onions and cabbage until softened.
2. Add apple, sugar and wine. Cook over low heat 1 to 1-1/2 hours (longer cooking increases mildness). May be cooked covered in an oven if cooking an oven meal for 1 hour; cook for 20 more minutes with the cover off.

PUMPERNICKEL RYE BREAD

3-1/2 to 4 cups white flour, sifted
2-3/4 cups rye flour, sifted
3 pkg dry yeast
1-1/2 cups warm water
1/4 cup molasses (a maybe)
4 t salt (a maybe)
1 to 3 T caraway seeds
2 T soft shortening

1. Sift the white and rye flours together. Set aside.
2. In a mixing bowl, dissolve the yeast in warm water. Add molasses, half of the flour, salt, caraway seeds and shortening. Beat with a spoon until smooth. Using your hands, mix the remaining flour until it cleans the bowl. Turn out onto a lightly floured board. Cover and let rest for 10 to 15 minutes. Knead for about 10 minutes.
3. Grease the bowl, including the sides. Place the plump piece of dough in the bowl and cover with a damp cloth. Let this rise in a nice warm place (about 85°) until it is double its size. This will take an hour.
4. Punch this down and let rise again, about 30 minutes. Then divide in half, shape into round loaves and let rest 10 to 15 minutes.
5. Shape loaves into round loaves again and put into greased pan. Let rise at least another hour. Bake 30 to 35 minutes in a 375° oven. This recipe yields 2 nice, round 9-inch loaves.

APPLE STREUSEL

(In German, this means apple crumb cake.)

---

6 medium-size peeled, cored and sliced cooking apples

---

2 T lemon juice

---

1 cup sugar

1/4 cup lukewarm water, 110-115°

---

1 pkg active dry yeast

1/4 t sugar

3/4 cup lukewarm milk

---

1 t finely grated lemon peel

1/3 cup sugar

---

1 egg, at room temperature

---

2 egg yolks, at room temperature

3-1/4 cups sifted all-purpose flour

---

7 T unsalted butter, softened

---

1 t cinnamon

1/2 t Crisco shortening

---

1. Mix the apple slices, lemon juice and sugar together, stirring to thoroughly coat apples. Set aside.
2. Pour lukewarm water into a small, shallow mixing bowl, and sprinkle it with yeast and 1/4 t sugar. (Sugar will activate the yeast.) Give the mixture a few minutes to activate and then stir to dissolve the yeast completely. After the yeast has doubled in volume, stir in the lukewarm milk and lemon peel.
3. In a large mixing bowl, beat the 1/3 cup sugar, the egg and the two egg yolks together. Then stir into the yeast mixture. Add 3 cups of the sifted flour, 1/2 cup at a time, beating after each additional 1/2 cup. Continue to beat until dough is soft and formed. Beat in 6 T soft butter, 1 T at a time.

4. Gather the dough into a ball and place onto a lightly floured surface. Knead this dough for approximately 10 minutes or until the dough is smooth and elastic, gradually adding the remaining 1/4 cup of flour to prevent the dough from sticking.
5. Again, gather the dough into a ball and place into a buttered bowl. Dust the top with flour. Cover the bowl with a towel and put into a warm, draft-free place and let rise until it is double its original size, approximately an hour and a half.
6. Preheat the oven to 375°. Lightly coat the bottom of a jelly roll pan with the Crisco. Set aside while you prepare streusel topping.

STREUSEL TOPPING

1/2 lb butter (2 sticks), cut into bits and thoroughly chilled

---

2 cups all-purpose flour

1-2/3 cup sugar

---

2 t ground cinnamon

1/4 cup melted butter

---

1. Prepare the streusel topping by combining the chilled butter bits, flour, sugar and 1 t of the cinnamon in a large bowl, working quickly.
2. Rub the flour and fat together with your fingertips until the mixture looks like flakes or crumbs of cake.
3. When the dough has risen, punch it down and knead it on a lightly floured surface for 5 minutes.
4. Place it on a jelly roll pan and stretch it out so that it covers the bottom of the pan.
5. Put the streusel mix evenly over the top of the cake and then place the sliced apples on top of this. Pour 1/4 cup melted butter over this. Sprinkle the remaining teaspoon of cinnamon on top.
6. Bake this on a rack set in the middle of the oven for 35 minutes, until the top is crusty. To serve, cut the cake into 2-inch squares and serve warm or at room temperature. This recipe will make one 11-by-17-inch cake.

PUMPKIN COOKIES

3 cups sugar
1 cup cooking oil
2 eggs
5 cups flour
1-1/2 t soda
1 t salt (a maybe)
1 cup crushed macadamia nuts
1 29-oz can pumpkin
2 T baking powder
5 t cinnamon
1 t vanilla
1 cup raisins

Mix the sugar, oil and eggs. Add pumpkin and stir in the dry ingredients. Add the vanilla, nuts and raisins. Bake at 350° for 15 minutes. Makes 8 to 10 dozen cookies, depending on their size.

POWDERED SUGAR FROSTING

(You will need to double this
for the pumpkin cookie recipe.)

---

3 T butter

1/2 cup brown sugar

1 cup powdered sugar

4 t milk

3/4 t imitation vanilla

---

1. Put 3 T butter into saucepan and add the brown sugar. Cook this until it is melted, stirring until completely dissolved. Add the powdered sugar, the vanilla and the milk.
2. If you frost the cookies while the frosting is hot, it will go on much smoother.

OCTOBER—ADULT HALLOWEEN PARTY:

Hors D'oeuvres
Crunchies

Beverage
Hot Apple Cider

Dessert
Cranberry Bread

Apple Dumplings

CRUNCHIES

You are on your own for this. They are simply your
favorite raw vegetables, sliced, on a platter.

HOT APPLE CIDER

1 qt apple cider
1 pt orange juice
1 pt cranberry juice
3/4 t whole cloves
1-1/2 sticks cinnamon
1-1/4 t whole allspice

1. Pour the cider, orange juice and cranberry juice into a percolator. Place the clove, cinnamon and allspice pieces in the basket.
2. Perk this as you would coffee. When the percolator stops, the cider is ready. Yields approximately 12 cups. (You may wish to double the recipe for a large crowd.)

CRANBERRY BREAD

2-1/2 cups all-purpose flour

1 cup milk

1/2 cup granulated sugar

1/2 cup brown sugar, packed

1/4 cup shortening

2 eggs

3 t baking powder

1/2 t salt

1/2 t baking soda

1 cup chopped cranberries

2 t grated orange peel

1 t lemon peel

2 t orange juice

1/4 cup shredded sharp cheddar cheese (optional; this is a maybe)

---

1. Mix the first ten ingredients together. Add the orange and lemon peels, the orange juice and cheddar cheese (if using).
2. Spread the mixture into a bread tin which has been greased with Crisco shortening and then floured. Bake for an hour at 350° or 375°, depending on your oven (some are hotter than others). It should bake on a rack in the center of the oven.
3. While the finished bread is still hot, take it out of the bread tin and frost it with powdered sugar frosting (recipe on page 326).

APPLE DUMPLINGS

---

2 cups flour
2 t baking powder
1/2 cup milk
1 t salt (a maybe)
3/4 cup Crisco shortening
4 to 6 medium-size apples, peeled and sliced (amount depends on how thick you roll the dough)
2 cups sugar
1/2 t cinnamon
1/4 cup butter
2 cups water
1/2 t nutmeg

1. Combine the flour, baking powder, and salt. Cut in the shortening. Add the milk and stir until just moist.
2. Roll 1/4-inch-thick squares.
3. Place the peeled apples on each square. Sprinkle with sugar. Fold around the apple and place the dumplings approximately an inch apart in a Crisco-greased pan.
4. Combine the sugar, cinnamon, butter, water and nutmeg in a saucepan. Cook over low heat for 5 minutes.
5. Pour the sugar syrup over the dumplings, and bake at 375° for 35 to 40 minutes. Remove from oven and either serve warm or cool the dumplings on a rack. Serve with cream if you can use it (a maybe for some people). This reheats very nicely.

NOVEMBER—THANKSGIVING:

Soup
Herbed Spinach Soup

Salad
Cranberry Molded Salad

Entree
Roast Turkey with Bread Stuffing

Jan's Grandmother's Cranberry Pudding

Mashed Potatoes and Gravy

Your Favorite Vegetables

Sweet Potatoes with Apple Rings

Dessert
Pumpkin Pie

HERBED SPINACH SOUP

3 green onions, finely chopped
2 T butter or margarine
4 qt chicken broth
3 sprigs parsley, finely chopped, or 1-1/2 t dried parsley
1 lb fresh spinach, well washed and cleaned
1/8 t pepper
1 t tarragon
1/2 cup light cream
1 hard-boiled egg, chopped

1. Sauté onions in melted butter or margarine until softened. Add chicken broth, parsley, spinach, pepper and tarragon. Cover and bring to boil, then lower heat and cook slowly for 45 minutes to 1 hour.
2. Remove from heat and pour into blender (a little at a time) and blend until vegetables are finely chopped.
3. Return blended mixture to pot. Bring to a boil and stir in cream. Lower heat and cook 15 to 20 minutes.
4. Remove to a soup tureen, garnish with chopped eggs and serve. Makes 8 servings.

ROAST TURKEY WITH BREAD STUFFING

---

1 10-lb turkey (Thaw the turkey a day ahead of time because it take a while to thaw completely. Start preparing the stuffing after the turkey is thawed.)

1/2 cup chopped onion

1/2 cup butter

---

1 t poultry seasoning or ground sage

1/2 t salt (a maybe)

1/8 t pepper

---

8 cups dry bread cubes

---

1 cup chicken broth, preferably homemade

---

vegetable oil

---

1. Cook the onion in butter until tender. Stir in seasonings.
2. In a large bowl, add onion mixture to the bread cubes. Pour broth or water over this and toss a little bit to mix the ingredients together. Put this aside and prepare your turkey.
3. Rinse turkey off and pat it dry. Rub cavity with salt (this is a maybe). Spoon some stuffing into the neck cavity and secure it by pulling the neck skin back over it. Spoon the remaining stuffing into the body cavity. Do not crowd it in because it will cook faster, easier and more evenly if you do not pack it.
4. Tuck the drumsticks into the band of skin at the tail. Tie the legs to the tail.
5. Place the bird in a grocery store brown bag, breast side up on a rack in a shallow roasting pan, brushed with vegetable oil. It does not require basting. Roast turkey in a 325° oven for a total of 4 to 4-1/2 hours. Usually, you roast a turkey for 20 minutes per pound.
6. After about 2-1/2 hours, when the bird is more than half done, cut the band or string between the legs to be sure that that part of the bird cooks. Before you carve it, let it sit for 15 minutes to let all the juices settle. It will then be easier to carve. This makes about 10 very healthy servings.

JAN'S GRANDMOTHER'S CRANBERRY PUDDING

---

1 cup frozen cranberries, cut in halves (It is easier to cut the berries in half while they are frozen.)

---

1 beaten egg

---

2 t sugar

1/2 cup light mild-flavored molasses

---

pinch salt

1/2 t brown sugar

1-1/2 cups flour

1-1/2 t baking soda

---

1 cup sugar

1/2 cup butter

---

2 t flour

---

1 cup cream (a maybe on your diet)

---

1. Bring 1/2 cup water to a boil, and dissolve 1-1/2 t baking soda in it. Mix together the cranberries, egg, sugar, molasses, salt, brown sugar and flour. Add the water and the baking soda to the mixture, and steam it in a double boiler for one hour. (One thing that is nice about this recipe is that you can keep it warm in the double boiler until you are ready to serve it. If it is finished in an hour, you can still hold it for 15, 20 or even 30 minutes longer if you just keep the water in the bottom of the double boiler and keep it steaming.)
2. While the mixture is steaming, mix the sugar, butter, flour and cream in a saucepan. Simmer, watching carefully and stirring when necessary so that the mixture does not burn on the bottom.
3. When you are ready to serve this, scoop the berry mixture out with a spoon and pour the sauce over it.

CRANBERRY MOLDED SALAD

1 pkg raspberry jello
1-3/4 cups very hot water
1/2 cup sugar
1 cup raw cranberries
1/2 cup celery
1 apple, unpeeled
1 medium orange, unpeeled
1/4 lemon, unpeeled

1. Mix together the jello, water and sugar. Stir well and let set until cold and slightly chilled.
2. Put the apple, orange and lemon through a food processor to chop up fine. Add the fruit, cranberries and celery to the jello. Put into a mold and chill. Serves approximately 6 people. This recipe can be doubled very easily.

MASHED POTATOES AND GRAVY

You can use your own favorite recipe for this. Use some of the turkey drippings for the gravy base. Season to taste as you please; there is nothing in particular that can bother anyone with migraine except for salt.

YOUR FAVORITE VEGETABLES

For your favorite vegetables, we suggest that you check our food list. Since we already have made some choices on this particular menu, we are going to leave that one up to you.

SWEET POTATOES
WITH APPLE RINGS

2 lb sweet potatoes, peeled

2 golden delicious apples, cored (one of the apples should be cut into rings and the other one should be chopped up)

salt

freshly ground pepper to taste

1/4 t ground cinnamon

4 T butter, cut into small pieces

2 T honey

2 T brown sugar

1/4 cup chopped macadamia nuts (a maybe)

1. The ideal situation would be to have a Cuisinart and use the french fry disc to run the sweet potatoes and the apple through. (You do not want to cut up the apple that was cut into the rings. You only want to chop up the remaining apple.) If you do not have a Cuisinart, however, just chop up the sweet potato and apple as fine as you can.
2. Sprinkle with salt, pepper and cinnamon and place in a buttered casserole dish.
3. Put the apple rings on top of this. Drizzle honey, sprinkle with brown sugar and dot with butter. Sprinkle macadamia nuts over top. Cover and bake at 350° for 45 minutes to an hour, till tender.

PUMPKIN PIE

Make a crust with your favorite recipe, using enriched flour for any flour called for.

Pie Filling

---

1 cup pumpkin (canned or fresh-cooked)

3/4 cup sugar

1/4 t salt

1 cup milk

2 eggs, separated (Beat egg whites until they form peaks.)

1 T melted butter

1 t ginger

1/2 t cinnamon

1/4 t cloves

Mix the above ingredients in order given, folding egg whites in last. Pour into the unbaked pie shell. Bake at 450° for 20 minutes. Turn oven to 350° and continue baking for 30 minutes.

DECEMBER—CHRISTMAS EVE SUPPER:

Salad
Avocado and Artichoke Salad

Bread
Corn Bread

Entree
Cajun Shrimp Stew

Dessert
Christmas Cookies

CAJUN SHRIMP STEW

1/4 cup celery, chopped
1 medium-size onion, chopped
1 clove garlic, crushed
4 T butter (1/2 stick)
1/3 cup sifted all-purpose flour
1/2 t thyme leaves, crumbled
salt to taste (a maybe)
1/2 t pepper
1 16-oz can tomatoes
1 14-oz can chicken broth
1 8-oz can minced clams
1/8 t liquid red pepper seasoning
1 16-oz can okra, drained
1 5-oz can shrimp, drained and rinsed (you may use about 1/2 lb fresh shrimp, but the fresh shrimp have to be boiled first)
3 cups cooked rice

1. Sauté the celery, onion and garlic in butter until soft. Stir in the flour and seasonings. Cook constantly until bubbly.
2. Stir in the tomato, homemade or canned chicken broth; clams, including the liquid that is in the can, and the red pepper seasoning. Continue to cook this until the mixture thickens and boils for 1 minute.
3. Add okra and shrimp and continue boiling.
4. Add rice. Reduce heat to simmer and continue to cook this until you are ready to serve it.

CORN BREAD

1-1/2 cups yellow cornmeal
2 cups sifted all-purpose flour (enriched)
2 T sugar
4 t baking powder
1 t salt (a maybe)
2 eggs
2 cups milk
4 T shortening

1. Combine cornmeal, flour, sugar, baking powder and salt in a large bowl and add eggs and milk. Stir to make a smooth batter. Add shortening.
2. Pour into two greased 8 by 2 inch baking pans. Bake in a hot oven (450°) for 25 minutes or until crusty and golden brown. Serve this warm. It makes approximately 16 servings.

AVOCADO AND ARTICHOKE SALAD

1 pkg lemon jello
1-3/4 cups hot water
1 T sugar
2 T ketchup
2 T vinegar
salt to taste
pepper to taste
1 ripe avocado, skinned, pitted and cut up
4 canned artichoke hearts, quartered

In a medium-size bowl, dissolve the jello in hot water and add the sugar, ketchup, vinegar, salt and pepper. Allow this to cool and thicken slightly, at which time you add the artichoke and avocado. Pour in a mold and refrigerate until thick.

AVOCADO/ARTICHOKE
SALAD DRESSING

1 cup mayonnaise
1/2 cup crab or shrimp
2 hard-boiled eggs, chopped
1/2 cup diced celery

Mix these ingredients together and use this as a topping for the Avocado and Artichoke Salad.

CHRISTMAS COOKIES

1 cup butter
1 cup granulated sugar
1 cup brown sugar, packed
4 eggs
3 T water
1 t imitation vanilla
1 t baking soda
1 t nutmeg
5 cups enriched flour, sifted
1 t salt (a maybe)

1. Cream the butter well. Add the white and brown sugars. In a separate bowl, beat the eggs and add the water and imitation vanilla.
2. Mix dry ingredients and add alternately with wet ingredients to the creamed butter and sugar.
3. Chill at least 1/2 hour before rolling out.
4. Roll the dough on a floured, cloth-covered board about 1/8 inch thick. Cut into fancy shapes or use cookie cutters. Bake in moderate oven (350°) for 8-10 minutes; remove from oven when golden on top. This recipe makes about 7 dozen cookies, depending on size. Decorate with frosting recipe which follows.

CHRISTMAS COOKIE FROSTING

4 T sugar
2 T water
1/4 t cream of tartar
2 egg whites
2/3 cup white vegetable shortening, preferably Crisco
1 t imitation vanilla
1 lb powdered sugar

1. Boil the sugar, water and cream of tartar for 1 minute.
2. Beat 2 egg whites.
3. Add hot syrup to the egg whites. Add the shortening, vanilla and powdered sugar.
4. Frost your Christmas cookies with this after they have cooled. Then decorate with colored sugar. This recipe is very good for decorating many cakes and cookies. It also freezes well if covered.

DECEMBER—CHRISTMAS DINNER:

Entree
Roast Beef with Yorkshire Pudding

Mashed Potatoes and Gravy

Green Beans with Basil

Cranberry Sauce Relish

Dessert
Mincemeat Turnovers

Beverage
Holiday Jewel

ROAST BEEF WITH YORKSHIRE PUDDING

4-6 lb boneless beef rump roast
2 T shortening
1 small onion, thinly sliced
4 eggs
2 cups milk
2 cups all-purpose enriched flour
2 t salt
1/2 cup roast beef pan drippings

1. Melt shortening in a heavy pan, and brown meat on all sides for a few minutes. Add onions; brown them.
2. Put the meat on a rack in the oven and bake at 325° until it has cooked sufficiently for your own taste (meaning rare, medium, or well done)— about 25 minutes per pound (2-1/2 hours for a 6-lb roast) for medium-cooked meat. When you place the meat on the rack, be sure that there is a pan underneath this rack to collect all the drippings for your Yorkshire Pudding.
3. While the meat is roasting, place the eggs and milk in a mixing bowl. Add the flour and salt (optional), and then beat the mixture for 2 minutes or until the batter is smooth.
4. Put about 1 tbsp of drippings into each cup of a muffin pan, and then pour the batter atop the drippings.
5. Bake in a 350° oven for about 20 to 30 minutes, until the pudding is golden brown. Watch carefully so that it does not get too brown and burn. If you do not wish to use muffin tins to make your Yorkshire Pudding, you can pour the drippings into a square cake pan and then pour your batter atop the drippings. Here again, you will bake the pudding at 350°, until it is golden brown. (This will take about 40 minutes.) When the pudding is done, turn off the oven and leave the pudding in to keep it warm until you are ready to serve; or remove from oven and serve immediately with your gravy-topped roast.

MASHED POTATOES AND GRAVY

Use your own recipe for this. You should use some of the drippings for the gravy. There is nothing in particular that can bother anyone with migraine except for salt.

GREEN BEANS WITH BASIL

2 T butter or margarine

1/2 t crushed dried basil

1 lb green beans, cleaned and cut, or 1 pkg french-style frozen green beans cooked in a small amount of water without salt.

Cook beans until tender but not mushy. Drain. Add butter and basil and serve. This is also a good way to serve italian green beans if these do not cause headaches.

CRANBERRY SAUCE RELISH

2 cups cranberries, chopped
1 whole orange, chopped
1 whole lemon, chopped
1/4 cup macadamia nuts, chopped

If you have a food processor, blender or food grinder, put all of the ingredients together in it. Mix to desired texture. Chill until ready to serve.

MINCEMEAT TURNOVERS

2 cups unbleached all-purpose flour

1/4 cup sugar

1 t baking powder

1/4 t salt

8 T butter, chilled and cut in small pieces

2 T lard, chilled and cut in small pieces

1/4 cup ice water

1 egg yolk, stirred to mix

1-1/4 cup canned pumpkin

1/3 cup prepared canned mincemeat

1/2 cup brown sugar

1 egg white with 1 t water for glaze

1 heaping t sugar

TIP: If you were to mix up the pastry and had a food processor, you would use a steel knife to do this. In fact, it is quite easy if you do have a processor. If you do not, just prepare your dough as you normally would, using the instructions which follow.

1. Sift the flour, sugar, baking powder and salt into a working bowl.
2. Place the chilled pieces of fat on top of the flour. Cut the fat into the flour until it resembles tiny peas.
3. Pour the ice water and egg yolk on top of this and just mix the dough until the ingredients are blended. Do not handle it any more that you have to.
4. Gather the dough on a piece of plastic wrap and press the dough into a rectangle. Wrap it well and refrigerate it for about an hour.
5. Place the pumpkin in a sieve to drain the liquid from it. (Otherwise, your turnover will be a little soggy.) Mix the sugar and the mincemeat with the pumpkin, using a large wooden spoon so that you do not chop up the mincemeat.

6. Remove the pastry from the refrigerator and roll half into a very thin rectangle. Cut into 4-inch circles with the cookie cutter. You should get about 8 circles out of this pastry.
7. Fill the pastry round with 1 T of pumpkin mixture. Moisten the rim of the pastry with water and then fold over the edge gently. Press it together with your thumb and forefinger. Seal with the tines of a fork.
8. Grease a large baking sheet with solid Crisco and place the turnovers on the sheet. Repeat instructions 6 and 7 to finish the other turnovers. Before you put these in the oven, brush the pastries with the egg white glaze and sprinkle with the sugar. Bake in a preheated 400° oven for about 20 minutes or until golden brown.

HOLIDAY JEWEL

1 oz vodka
6 oz cranberry juice (approx.)
1 lime wedge

For each drink, fill an old-fashioned glass with ice cubes. Add vodka. Fill with cranberry juice. Stir, and garnish with lime wedge.

Dining Out

DINING OUT

Congratulations! At this point you have traveled a long way down the road to managing your migraine headaches. You have read the first chapters of this book and gained a better understanding of the migraine process and its most common triggers. Perhaps with the help of your physician, you have analyzed your life style and increased your awareness of the events and substances which trigger your own headaches. You have determined that a careful diet plays a major role in preventing your attacks. Finally, you have studied and worked with the food lists and recipes to achieve a good degree of dietary control in your own home.

You are ready now to meet the challenge of dining out without fear of losing control of your diet. You can enjoy one of America's favorite pastimes and remain migraine-free. Careful planning is your key to success.

The Stress Mess to Avoid

Once you have accomplished a successful dietary regimen at home, you could find that dining out—unprepared—is one of the most uncomfortable experiences you can imagine. Picture yourself in the following scene.

Because you are more aware of how your body reacts to certain foods, you naturally would prefer to avoid ordering those foods when eating at a restaurant. Unfortunately, you may be unable to find a suitable choice among the items which are offered. Even when a dish does seem appropriate, you find yourself wondering precisely what ingredients are used in its preparation. At this point you may become frustrated, uncertain how to proceed. Your stress level is rising; you are afraid the tension might trigger a migraine before you even order your food! Panicking, you decide that the only way out is to abandon your diet and order quickly whatever you love the most. Although that dish could be the worst possible choice, by now you are willing to suffer a headache rather than continue the nightmare of inner conflict. Defeated by your loss of control, you wonder hopelessly how soon the pain will begin; will you even be able to finish your meal? This may sound all too familiar. But from now on, you should remember that there is an alternative to the unwanted headaches. We have outlined a few suggestions that may help.

1. *Know your limitations.* The first strategy we recommend is learning all you can about your own food and chemical triggers. Until you are

thoroughly familiar with the food list that works for you, we suggest that you take the one in this book with you when you are dining out.

2. *Simplify your choices ahead of time.* As we have stated before and emphasize again: planning ahead is paramount. You will derive a good deal more pleasure from your outing if choosing your meal is as simple as possible. This is easy if you are well acquainted with the restaurant where you will be dining. Evaluate the menu in your mind before you arrive and plan what you will order.

If you are unsure about some of the ingredients, you might telephone ahead and ask to speak to someone who can help you. Most restaurant personnel will accomodate you if they realize that you need information for your health maintenance. The advantages of telephoning are that you demonstrate courtesy to the staff and allow yourself time to be prepared. This approach is a particularly good one if you will be visiting an unfamiliar restaurant.

3. *Take the time you need.* What should you do if you find yourself on your way out the door for a spontaneous feast? Do not let the unexpected element of the occasion catch you off guard. Most eating establishments will have at least one entree that you will recognize as safe. If necessary, depending on your will power, order only salad. Remember that you have the right to ask your waiter or waitress what ingredients are used in preparing the dish you would like to order. If need be, ask that the chef assist you in obtaining the information you should have to make a good, safe choice. This is not a time to be weak or to feel rushed; you must be assertive to manage your health and well-being. If you realize that the very worst possibility is that you may have to leave politely, it is obvious that remaining free of pain is worth the price.

4. *Keep general guidelines in mind.* A general rule for all migraine patients who believe that diet control is an important element of their lives is to be prepared to pass up the customary hors d'oeuvres, desserts and after-dinner drinks, particularly until you feel like an expert on what you should eat.

Another good idea is to consume less of your known problem foods during the day or so before you dine out.

Try to consider the combination of foods you will be eating. Think of your meal as a time to balance items that you know to be safe—eat a maximum of these—with a minimum of problem or questionable ones. This technique will enable you to dilute your potential sources of trouble.

5. *Plan support.* Any discipline is easier to maintain when you have supportive friends or family around you. If you attempt to follow your diet while dining away from home and you are in the company of people with whom you do not feel entirely comfortable, you may put yourself in an awkward position. Consider how you will deal with acquaintances who do not understand your condition. Perhaps you would prefer to keep your diet to yourself. You may not wish to explain that you are vitally interested in every morsel you put in your mouth. In this case, it may be advisable to invite one or two close friends or family members who know and understand your situation to accompany you for your first meals out. Their support could turn the occasion into a victory for everyone.

6. *Develop a positive mental attitude.* As you strive to meet the challenge of eating to stay healthy and migraine-free, remember that being proud of regulating your own life, building on each success, no matter how small, and gaining confidence in your dietary control of your migraine are your most important goals.

Fast Foods

Many of us today rely on the convenience of fast food establishments, at least occasionally. If you frequent such places as Kentucky Fried Chicken, McDonald's, Burger King or Arthur Treacher's Fish and Chips, keep in mind that most of these eateries use ingredients such as monosodium glutamate (MSG). This chemical is one of the migraine patient's worst enemies. To keep yourself out of danger of a migraine attack, we recommend that you pay careful attention to the above strategies.

First of all, keep your limitations foremost in your mind. The convenience of the quick meal is not worth a full-blown migraine. Second, take your time in deciding what to order. This approach will also pay dividends in your return visits because the menu changes infrequently in most such restaurants. Third, combine your foods carefully so that you can dilute any quantity of a problem chemical or food you consume. For example, you might order a hamburger or a fish sandwich instead of a cheeseburger if you should avoid cheese. Rather than drinking milk, a milkshake or a soft drink, it would be wise to choose coffee, tea or juice. Leave out the french fries, which are usually loaded with salt.

We have found in our research that Burger King will prepare your hamburger on the grill just as you request it. Another positive trend is the addition of salad bars in many fast food places; salads provides a safe and delicious way to vary your menu within the necessary guidelines.

Ethnic/Exotic Foods

When delving into ethnic dining without advance planning, you will always be taking a risk. We cannot emphasize enough the caution you should exercise. If you will be sampling exotic cuisine, by all means try to think out your choices ahead of time.

German—If you were to try a German restaurant, you might find sauerkraut, a variety of sausages, and Bavarian beers. Germans are also renowned for their wild game marinated for hours in cream sauce and red wine. Rather than be discouraged by these off-limit selections, look more carefully at the array of foods. You will find such permissible delicacies as spaetzle (fresh noodles) and beef, which are great with homemade rolls and fresh vegetables.

Italian—If you patronize an Italian eatery, you could enjoy their minestrone soup; ask about the spices first. It is a well-known fact that the Italians like to spice up their foods but they also like to do it naturally, so we would not expect to find MSG on their spice racks. They use cheese in most of their dishes but it is usually added at the end of the preparation and can be easily eliminated upon request.

Pasta itself is fine. Its ingredients are flour, eggs, and water. Oil is also added, but usually not enough to make a difference. Because most of the sauces are heavily salted, you should consider a sauce as your only salt consumption for the evening. The meat selection with the pasta is individual, so that is simple. You know which meats are not allowed.

If you order antipasto (salad), leave the salami, anchovies and olives on the platter. A pizza would not be easy to order; the crust is often baked in olive oil and then smothered in everything from sausages to olives and cheese.

Mexican—You will be delighted to learn that the cuisine of Mexico is mostly acceptable as is. What needs to be eliminated can be done easily; however, many of the staple foods (such as corn) are good for you. Dehydrated masa flour is made and then used in the tortilla, taco and enchilada. Burritos are made from wheat flour.

Fillings are simple to choose if you always remember to exclude sour cream, cheese and pork. Avocados are great when prepared in real Mexican style guacamole, not the California recipe using cream cheese and sour cream. Chilies and pinto beans are "maybes" on our food list, so you need to explore and learn what your limits are here. If the salsa (mild picante sauce) is prepared without olive oil, it should be no problem.

A favorite Mexican dish of ours is the traditional paella, consisting of rice, vegetables and whatever seafood is readily available. Some recipes do call for sausage and chicken and, of course, you would have to do without the sausage.

The Mexicans are very creative in preparing you a feast fit for a king—but then, why not? Their ideas originated in part with the Spanish conquistadores who invaded Mexico in the early 1500s.

French—I would warn those of you who are tempted by the delicacies of the French to proceed with great caution! Their food is classically prepared with generous amounts of cream, butter and wine—devastating!

Pacific Northwestern Cuisine—The hardy Northerners tend to feast on the blessings of the sea, fields and streams. What a variable selection most suitable for your diet! The only time seafood should be a problem is when it is smoked, such as smoked salmon. We would suggest, too, that you try the Manhattan clam chowder with its tomato base instead of the New England with its cream and cheese. Note that a few slices of bacon are used for flavor, but not enough to do any real harm.

Steak Houses—It is our opinion that the steak houses which are found in all parts of the country are a safe refuge. Usually you can find foods which are prepared in your presence. This makes it easy to request any changes or substitutions. As an extra bonus, you can sample a wide variety of salads, potatoes and other vegetables.

Oriental Foods—Japanese food is probably easier on the migraine person than Chinese food. The chief offender in Japanese cooking is not MSG, but rather miso, a very salty derivative of soy beans used as a flavoring. Avoid the clear fish soups and the pickled salads, especially on an empty stomach. Try a family-run restaurant until you are familiar with the various dishes, and then branch out. If there are no family-run restaurants available, then a Benihana's is a good place to start since the meal is prepared while you watch.

With Chinese cooking it is really a good idea to know your ingredients and your restaurant. MSG is, of course, the best-known migraine trigger, but soy sauce is equally deadly since it is loaded with salt. Again avoid the clear soups—go for the more hardy ones or skip the soup course. No doubt your best migraine protection when eating Oriental foods is to ask about the use of MSG. We recently ate in a Mongolian Barbecue where they advertised that their sauces were made without MSG. So don't be shy; ask and protect yourself.

SUMMARY

In conclusion, I would like to say that throughout our search for a better understanding of the headache problem, we interviewed and followed the progress of a number of patients under the care of Dr. William Stump and Dr. Sander Bergman, neurologists. We gave them our food list of no-no's and monitored their intake as closely as possible. We were not at all surprised to find that our Italian patient had eliminated a large number of her headaches by reducing the amount of cheddar cheese she used on a daily basis. She readily admits that if she cheats and indulges in no-no's on the list, she can almost always count on a headache. If she realizes she has cheated, she tries to correct the tyramine imbalance with other positive foods, to counteract the headache-triggering process. She says that this doesn't always work, but admits that these are the times she'll never forget.

Another monitored patient mentions that when she weakens and has a hot fudge sundae, she is fully aware of its outcome, has a migraine from it, and later, of course, regrets having had the taboo food.

Some physicians claim that by putting patients on a migraine diet, along with monitoring their life styles (meaning more sleep and less stress, if possible), they have gradually reduced the frequency of their headaches. Often when patients are asked what they feel is most responsible in their success at controlling migraines, they immediately state diet. We hope that with a little knowledge, effort, guidance and the supervision of a physician, you too can succeed in using diet to help control your headaches.

Subject Index

Recipe Index